A Play About Time Travel (Or Whatever)

by Zachary Olson

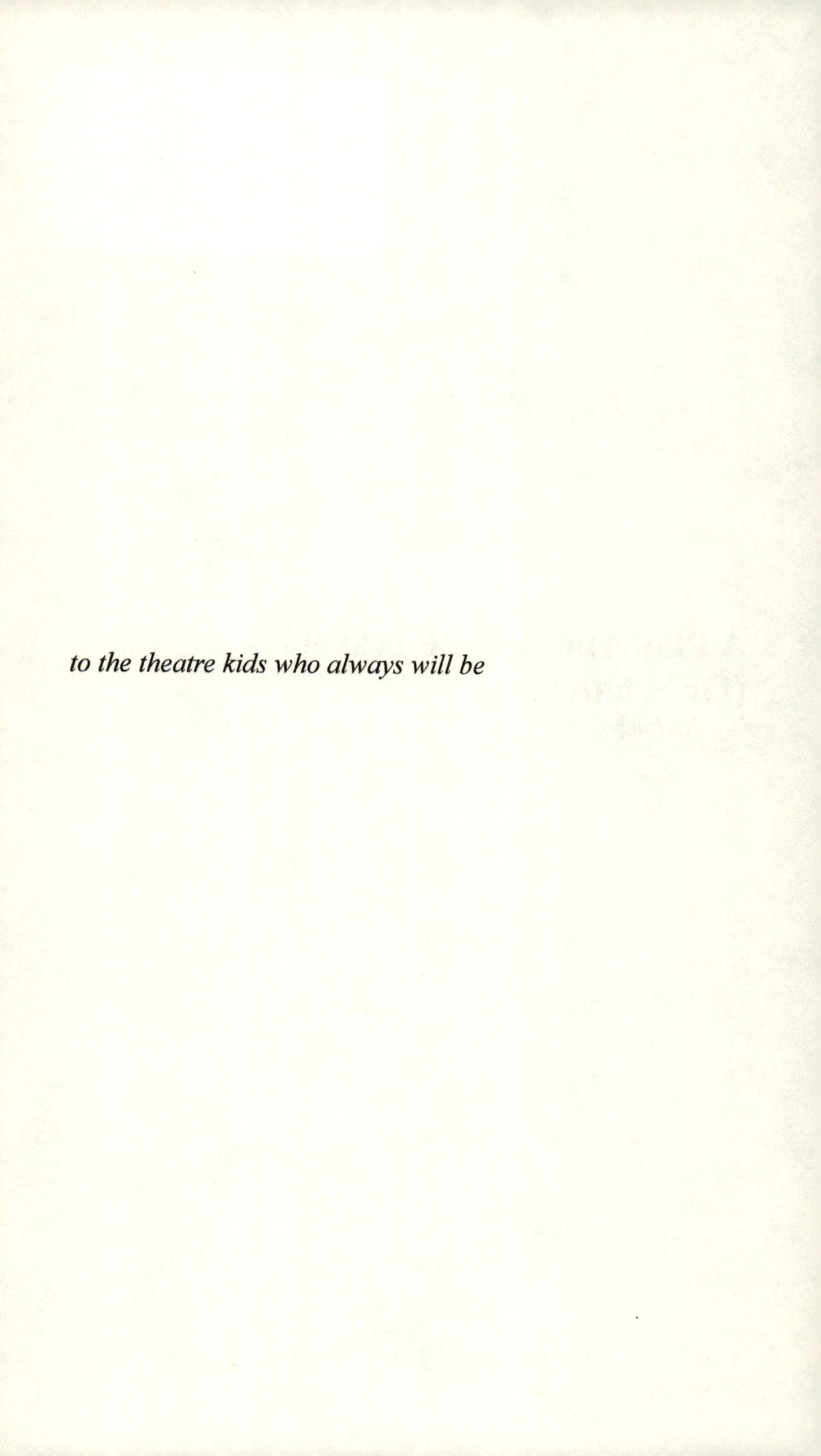

to the theatre kids who always will be

LICENSING & PRODUCTION INQUIRIES
Uproar Theatrics, LLC.
hello@uproartheatrics.com I www.UproarTheatrics.com

CHARACTERS

STAGE MANAGER/SIENNA:
Senior. Organized and efficient. A powerhouse. The stage manager of *The Winter Play* and a narrator of *A Play About Time Travel (Or Whatever)*. Wears all black in a distinctly different style than ASSISTANT STAGE MANAGER, maybe a walkie-talkie headset, and always has a clipboard or notebook - except at the New Year's Eve party. Unless indicated, she speaks directly to the audience.

ASSISTANT STAGE MANAGER:
Sophomore. Young, but competent. The assistant stage manager of *The Winter Play* and a narrator of *A Play About Time Travel (Or Whatever)*. Wears all black in a distinctly different style than STAGE MANAGER, maybe a walkie-talkie headset, and carries at least one roll of tape or broom at all times - except at the New Year's Eve party. Unless indicated, she speaks directly to the audience.

CAITLIN/MS. GUTIERREZ:
Sophomore. Anxious, but determined. She has noticeable character growth that shows in body language and confidence. In the end, she has arrived somewhere she never knew she could be. She wears a zip-up gray hoodie and often has an overstuffed sidebag. Best friends with SETH. Plays *THE LEAD* in *The Winter Play*. In the final scene, MS. GUTIERREZ has costume elements that connect back to CAITLIN.

BRITNEY:
Senior. Confident, but entitled. A wannabe social media influencer. She is an experienced and talented actor who has gotten the leads in previous shows. She has noticeable character growth that shows in body language and attitude - but it's still difficult for her to adjust. In the end, she arrives in a better place. Very fashionable, she likes baby blue.

Dating SCOTTY. Plays *THE LOVE INTEREST'S MOTHER* in *The Winter Play*.

MS. MAE:
Dedicated, resourceful theatre and creative writing teacher. She's been doing this a while, has seen it all, and loves it. She always wears something purple and has a name badge hanging around her neck when at school. Mid 30s-40s.

SETH:
Sophomore. Supportive, no questions asked. He's finding his way optimistically. Best friends with CAITLIN. He is the Assistant House Manager and a tech kid for life!

LEVI:
Senior. A powerhouse. The light in every room. Often wears a jean jacket of some kind. His drag alter ego is MS. JANE AUSTEN TEXAS. Plays *THE NARRATOR* in *The Winter Play*.

SCOTTY:
Senior. He is the ultimate sports-bro and new to theatre. He wears athletic clothing, usually shorts. Dating BRITNEY. Plays *THE LOVE INTEREST* in *The Winter Play*.

HARLOW:
Senior. Wears thick-framed cat-eye glasses and fun eyeliner. Very experienced and organized House Manager. They are nonbinary [cast accordingly where possible].

JACOB:
Sophomore. Lovable, foolish, doesn't read social cues. Probably wears a corny t-shirt with a cartoon on it. Plays *THE TENNIS PLAYER* in *The Winter Play*.

NORA:
Junior transfer student who is still figuring out how to fit in.
She's a good actor. Plays *THE LEAD'S MOTHER* in *The
Winter Play*.

CYNTHIA:
Junior. Shy, but reliable actor who shines onstage. Initially
plays *THE NEWSPAPER BOY* in *The Winter Play*.

TEAGAN:
Junior. Really bad at accents, but uses them all the time. Best
friends with OLIVIA. Plays *THE MILKMAN* in *The Winter
Play.*

OLIVIA:
Junior. Best friends with TEAGAN. Plays *THE SCIENTIST*
in *The Winter Play.*

CAITLIN'S LITTLE BROTHER:
Literally the *worst*. But really not that bad. 6-12 years old.
[Could be played by the same actor as one of the
STUDENTS, should appear younger than CAITLIN.]

CAITLIN'S MOM:
Supportive and loving, but a bit distant. Workaholic lawyer.
Mid 40s-50s.

CAITLIN'S DAD:
Supportive dad, sometimes too supportive. He's a pharmacist
and loves science. Mid 40s-50s.

LEVI'S MOM:
Loves and supports LEVI. Works at their church. Mid
40s-50s. [Could be played by the same actor as CAITLIN'S
MOM or a STUDENT.]

P.E. TEACHER:
A stereotype. Knee-high socks and short shorts. Mustache?
Mid 40s-60s. [Could be played by the same actor as
CAITLIN'S DAD, CAITLIN'S MOM, LEVI'S MOM, or a
STUDENT.]

STUDENTS:
A chorus of freshmen. Enthusiastic newcomers to the tech
crew who are eager to learn and contribute. They worship
SIENNA as their leader. They are many, they are one. This
can be a dedicated group depending on the size of casting
needs, or it can be played with the named characters. They
wear similar, plain clothes that will allow them to be not
distracting in the background when needed.

<u>CASTING</u>
- This is an inclusive script and casting should reflect
  that. While pronouns are indicated throughout, all
  characters are flexible and can be evolved to reflect
  the actor chosen for the role.
- If names need to change, choose something close to
  the original.

<u>SETTING</u>
- Present day at any high school in any town.
- Flexible. It can be simple or as detailed as you
  choose.
- There is no need for a full set, just chairs/stools and
  props as needed to make the scenes pop. Mime
  where you feel like it works.
- Experiment with using the STUDENTS as a way to
  shape some of the needed spaces such as the hallway
  in Act 1/Scene1.

<u>**SOUND AND VOICES**</u>
- As much as possible, the sound effects and background musical interludes should be provided live onstage by STUDENTS.
- All accent usage is meant to be funny and non-offensive. Adjust any accents to fit your specific community and what they will find the most enjoyable.

<u>**COSTUMES**</u>
- Everyday clothes are modern and each character might have a unique look, perhaps a signature color or pattern, but it doesn't need to be too blatant.
- Characters should wear the same outfit throughout, except where indicated and during:
  - The New Year's Eve party where they should be dressed festively (think sparkles!)
  - It's suggested that the costumes worn by characters during the production of *The Winter Play* are from the range of the 1800s-1960s. Get creative with what you have in your closet already! The era doesn't really matter, it just needs to be consistent for the whole cast of *The Winter Play* and contrast with the modern vibe in the rest of the show.
  - During the production of *The Winter Play*, actors should be in costumes appropriate to their *The Winter Play* characters. If you want to fill in the stage with some STUDENTS and they don't have a named *The Winter Play* character, have some fun with it, but stay within the era. Perhaps a farmer, a mailman, a golfer, a plumber, etc. You do you.

<u>**BLOCKING/ACTION**</u>

- During narrated portions, the actions described are acted out according to your discretion, unless otherwise indicated.
- Set changes are fluid and most scenes should flow immediately into the next as quickly and smoothly as possible.
  - This will require well structured lighting areas onstage and actors (STUDENTS mostly) to do set changes as scenes are happening in different areas of the stage.

<u>**ACT 1 / SCENE 1 - The Cast List**</u>

Location: Car, Classroom, Gym, Performing Arts Hallway

(Blank stage. STAGE MANAGER and ASSISTANT STAGE MANAGER move around, interacting with the audience as seems fit. They are always working on something.

The car can be represented symbolically rather than literally. This can be achieved with stools or chairs arranged to suggest a car, or by having the characters stand in a formation that implies a car. CAITLIN is always the central focus, with CAITLIN'S MOM and CAITLIN'S LITTLE BROTHER positioned in the car with her.)

STAGE MANAGER

(Standing to one side.)
Caitlin Gutierrez climbed into her parents' candy apple red minivan and supremely struggled to get to the furthest backseat. Her annoying little brother hurried in after her, competing for the same seat but settling for the middle row when he realized he was no match for her. Caitlin hugged her side bag, which she left attached under the seat belt. She pulled her puffy jacket over the whole situation - resulting in a very large mound of what she claimed was her fair territory.

CAITLIN

This is my fair territory!

(CAITLIN'S LITTLE BROTHER crosses his arms in defeat.)

1

CAITLIN'S LITTLE BROTHER
Okay, fine, whatever.

ASSISTANT STAGE MANAGER
(Stepping out from the other side, or she's already there and the lighting comes up.)
No one in her family knew yet, but she had tried out for the school play two days earlier. Today, the cast list would be posted and she was only about forty percent sure she wasn't going to puke at any given moment.

SM
She had helped with backstage tech stuff for two of the plays last year.

ASM
One of them was a musical too.

SM
But over the summer and the first few months of school, she had secretly psyched herself up to audition for an onstage role in *The Winter Play*. Top secret…

SM/ASM
…no way anyone could find out.

SM
It's not that her parents disapproved, quite the opposite in fact. She knew, just *knew* they would be super annoying and warm fuzzy supportive.

ASM
It was embarrassing and there was no way she was going to tell them.

CAITLIN

I - uh - might go over to Seth's house today after school.
Don't need you to pick me up.

SM

This was, of course, a lie.

CAITLIN'S MOM

Okay, sounds good!

ASM

She was just crafting an alibi for the *slightest* chance she got
cast in the show and needed to go to the script read-through
after school. Seth was always a great excuse.

> *(The characters, except CAITLIN, involved in
> the car formation peel off and disappear. SETH
> appears out of nowhere, all smiles, a few feet to
> the side of CAITLIN. SETH and CAITLIN speak
> towards, but not to the audience.)*

SETH

I'm a great excuse! (*Waves enthusiastically.*)

ASM

He lived next to the school and...

SETH

...we've been friends since second grade and it isn't...

CAITLIN

...weird or...

SETH

...mushy or...

CAITLIN
…gross and it would *never* be like that.

SM
They were friends forever and it was…

SM/ASM/CAITLIN/SETH
…perfect.

> *(CAITLIN and SETH give each other a high five or a secret handshake and the lights change. Any number of STUDENTS appear and create a clear classroom formation. CAITLIN, as always, is the central focus.)*

SM
Sitting through six periods felt especially agonizing.

CAITLIN
This is especially agonizing.

> *(On the following line, each of the STUDENTS hold up a sheet of paper in crisp unison and "staple" it on "the bulletin board" in front of them. Each STUDENT makes a stapling noise. The sheet of paper could either be blank or have "CAST LIST" written on the top followed by the actual cast list for your play - get as detailed as you want. Every time "cast list" is mentioned in the rest of this scene, STUDENTS repeat it in a whisper from wherever they are.)*

SM
She pictured the cast list going up on the bulletin board at the end of the performing arts hallway, her name nowhere to be seen *(STUDENTS look desperately for their names on the cast list they are holding.)*, shame brought to her family…

STUDENTS
(Shaking the paper held with one hand at the top where it is "stapled" and whispering.)
Shameeee....

SM
...a curse from a local witch settling upon her for the rest of eternity.

(A thunder/lightning moment or other dramatic light/sound effect reveals a stereotypical witch cackling in the background or to the side, very visible and very evil. CAITLIN is the only one who sees the witch and reacts.)

ASM
In the least dramatic sense, it felt like her guts were...

CAITLIN
...repeatedly tripping down stairs.

(CAITLIN acknowledges a stomach ache. The school bell rings.)

SM
The bell finally rang after fifty-five of the...

CAITLIN
...longest minutes of my *life*...

(On the word "volleyball," STUDENTS crumple up the sheet of paper and spike it dramatically off stage or into the audience, whatever feels most fun. It's a missed opportunity if at least one of the STUDENTS doesn't do a jump spike over the "net" with the crumpled paper.)

SM

…playing volleyball. The P.E. teacher never allowed them to prop the side door open for fresh air, and today she felt especially clammy.

P.E. TEACHER

(Stepping out.)
The feral cats'll get in. You want rabies, do yuh?

(STUDENTS meow.)

ASM

Or maybe it was raccoons. Caitlin's mind had been elsewhere.

SM

Even though she was anxious to check the cast list, she decided to shower.

(Most STUDENTS exit.)

CAITLIN

(Smelling herself.)
I should shower.

> *(SUGGESTED TRANSITION: Several girl*
> *STUDENTS walk by from either side of stage,*
> *shaking out towels and blocking CAITLIN*
> *during the following line before exiting.)*

ASM

The shower line wasn't long, but it still took a good twenty minutes because this was just the sort of thing Caitlin was slow at.

> *(CAITLIN, with a towel wrapped around her "wet" hair, adjusts her side bag and sets off towards the performing arts building. A few STUDENTS pass CAITLIN on her walk, but most are gathered outside the building, several of them dabbing at runny mascara, audibly crying, etc. The way they are configured helps define the space.)*

CAITLIN

(To herself.)
That's about to be me.

> *(CAITLIN struggles her way through the heavy main doors and down the hallway. The space is defined by STUDENTS. BRITNEY stands out along the way with a sour look.)*

And *that* is a death glare.

> *(STUDENTS each shout something at CAITLIN at the same time. It's maybe a congratulations of some kind, but it's not totally understandable. CAITLIN is confused by STUDENTS' shouts, gestures to them for clarification, but shrugs when she doesn't get any.)*

Freshmen.

(Shakes her head.)

SM

They were still recovering from middle school.

> *(CAITLIN sets her bag down off to the side and makes her way center stage to the cast list. The lighting focuses to highlight a single sheet of*

paper posted on an oversized bulletin board, possibly held by some of the STUDENTS. It should clearly say "CAST LIST" above or on the paper. This could be a good place to have some dramatic music/sound escalate - opera could work nicely. CAITLIN is frozen in front of the cast list, her finger pointing to the bottom of it.)

                    CAITLIN
(Getting discouraged.)
Nothing. *Nothing.*

                    ASM
She could feel her fingers going numb and her stomach churning.

        (STUDENTS start up a chant of "cast list" - hushed, but escalating.)

                    BRITNEY
(Snipping out the words. This is not a natural thing for her to say.)
Congrats. I guess.

                    CAITLIN
(Confused.)
What are you talking about?

        (CAITLIN, fighting back tears, circles back to face BRITNEY, who stands with her arms crossed. BRITNEY points past CAITLIN to the top of the cast list.)

                    BRITNEY
Look at the top of the list, dummy.

*(CAITLIN turns, her finger slowly tracing up the
cast list. STUDENTS' chant escalates until she
reaches the top. Pause.)*

STUDENTS
*(In crisp unison, elongating the end of the line until it fades
out.)*
Caitlin Gutierrez.

CAITLIN

The lead role?

BRITNEY

The lead role.

STUDENTS

The lead role.

SM

As a sophomore.

ASM

Caitlin was about to throw up.

CAITLIN

I'm about to what?

*(CAITLIN turns to the audience, gags, and
"throws up" all over her shoes. Black out.)*

<u>**ACT 1 / SCENE 2 - Main Character Energy**</u>
Location: Anywhere

*(BRITNEY stands center on a blank stage,
"recording" each segment with her phone.
Lighting is focused on each new area where she
moves.)*

BRITNEY

Britney here!
Sooo. Auditions for the next play are this week.
The lead role is perfect for me.
Ms. Mae is going to *love* what I have planned for the
character.
I was *made* for this one, you guys.
Anyways, talk soon!

*(BRITNEY moves to a new part of the stage.
During this next segment, SCOTTY joins for the
next video with BRITNEY. His outfit is very
sporty and he has a significant sling on one of
his arms. He is holding a football or helmet
under his other arm.)*

BRITNEY

Britney here!
You know my boyfriend, Scotty!

(BRITNEY drags SCOTTY into the shot.)

You *guysss*, he threw out his shoulder at football this week.

SCOTTY

It's really painful.

BRITNEY

He's benched for the rest of the season.

> *(SCOTTY poorly throws the football or helmet off side stage with a big frown. SM might catch it.)*

It took some convincing, but I got him to *audition* for the play!!

> *(On the previous line, SCOTTY gives a giant smile and a big thumbs up with both hands. He winces at the pain. SCOTTY runs off stage. OPTIONAL: STUDENTS can lean in from off stage and whisper "cast list" real quick when it's mentioned during the following dialogue.)*

BRITNEY

Britney here.
The cast list got posted today!
Scotty got cast as the *main* character's love interest.
And I'm *so* proud of him!

SCOTTY

(SCOTTY runs across the stage through the video shot, brushing off a shoulder with overconfidence.)
Got that main character *energy*, bay-bee!

BRITNEY

Cute. *Great*.
But I did *not* get the main character.

> *(SCOTTY frowns.)*

I'm playing Scotty's mother.

> *(BRITNEY and SCOTTY both cringe.)*

BRITNEY and SCOTTY

Not cute.

SCOTTY

Not *great.*

BRITNEY

No one should have to be their boyfriend's mother.

SCOTTY

(Sticking his tongue out and shaking his head.)
Disgusting.

> *(During the next recording, SCOTTY awkwardly exits.)*

BRITNEY

(In one breath, her hands gripping the phone tightly as she "records." This video is more of a confessional.)
You guys, I'm pretty sure Scotty is going to fall in love with Caitlin. You *know* it always happens with the leads in every play ever and I am going to lose my boyfriend of two years right before senior prom and I'll have to go alone like an absolute loser!

> *(Pause. Big, elongated breath. During the breath, SM and ASM attempt to retake possession of the stage, perhaps with a broom or vacuum in tow to simply do their jobs. But on the word "disaster," they understand it is not worth it and flee in opposite directions offstage.)*

This is a *disaster* and the worst thing that's ever or *will* ever happen to me and my life is essentially *over!* Why didn't I get the role I was born to play? Why did a sophomore techie like *Caitlin Gutierrez* get the lead? She's never been

BRITNEY (cont)

onstage in her *life*. Ms. Mae did this on *purpose*. *(Pathetic, exhausted.)* How could she hate me so much?

(Lights out as BRITNEY swooshes offstage.)

<u>ACT 1 / SCENE 3 - The Night Before</u>
Location: Ms. Mae's Apartment

(ASM stands center stage with a neat but clearly handmade cardboard sign that says "The Previous Night" and then adds an additional, smaller sign that says "The Theatre Teacher's Home." ASM exits, revealing MS. MAE standing center stage in pajamas and a purple bathrobe. She holds up a wine glass and dramatically pours a very full glass of chocolate milk, which she then drinks in one satisfying go. She hands the glass and milk jug to SM, who takes it off stage.

A large bulletin board "murder board" comes into view on one side, it should have a big title across the top that says "CAST LIST." The board is covered in photos and names [use real cast/crew member photos], a web of red string, and perhaps post-it notes with a lot of question marks. MS. MAE inspects it, but seems dissatisfied. She flips the bulletin board over or pulls out a second board from behind that looks even more wild. Feel free to do this a third time if desired, whatever works and is ridiculous. The bulletin boards could be on wheels or held by STUDENTS.

*MS. MAE is displeased. There is a noticeable
gap missing on the first board. SM pops out of
nowhere and hands MS. MAE a stack of
oversized photos. MS. MAE takes the photos, but
never acknowledges SM. MS. MAE has the slight
undertone of a mad scientist in this scene.)*

MS. MAE

Who do I choose? The underclassman?

*(SM nods vigorously to herself and runs off or
drops back behind something.)*

Yesss. Exactly.

(MS. MAE shuffles through the photos.)

Fresh, raw talent. Experience is great, but believability is
even better. This isn't a flashy show, it requires an
understated talent, a hidden power.

SM

(Reappearing.)
This was the worst part of the job - the inevitable
disappointment some students would face no matter what
choices Ms. Mae made.

ASM

(Appearing.)
She wished, as always, that she could give each of them the
lead.

MS. MAE

Go with your gut.

*(MS. MAE dances over to the first bulletin board
and slams CAITLIN's photo onto the noticeable*

*gap. This triumphant dance can be as elaborate
as desired - a dance break perhaps?)*

SM

Her gut had never been wrong before.

(Lights out with a flourish.)

<u>ACT 1 / SCENE 4 - The Script Read-Through</u>
Location: The Stage

*(SETH stands on stage, holding his phone at an
angle away from his ear as a series of high
pitched shrieks and heavy breathing emanates
from CAITLIN on the other end, who is currently
onstage and in place opposite SETH, but not lit
yet. After a moment, SM arrives and sits on the
edge of the stage to speak to the audience
between CAITLIN's deranged, unintelligible
noises on the phone. SM may need to speak
louder at times to be heard above CAITLIN. It
should be comical. SCOTTY still has a sling on
in this scene.)*

SM

Seth had already seen the cast list. He knew Caitlin had
gotten the lead role. And his name was on there too. He was
the Assistant House Manager and happy to be working
behind the scenes.

SETH
*(Covering the phone's speaker with his hand and
holding it away from his ear, but CAITLIN's
ruckus can still be heard. To the audience.)*
I'm a tech kid through and through!

(Some STUDENTS pop in.)

STUDENTS

(Sing-songy, with jazz hands.)
Seth's a tech kid through and through!

ASM

This meant he got to work with Harlow, who was the House
Manager for the sixth time in a row. And Harlow knew
exactly what they were doing.

HARLOW

*(Pops in holding a clipboard or something, waves at the
audience, maybe a salute.)*
I'm Harlow and I know exactly what I'm doing.

(Some STUDENTS pop in.)

STUDENTS

(Sing-songy, with jazz hands.)
Harlow knows exactly what they're doing!

(STUDENTS, and then HARLOW, pop back out.)

SETH

(Speaking on the phone.)
Caitlin, take a sec and *breathe*! You're going to pass out. I'm
just walking back from the vending machine, I got you a
cookie. *(He holds it up.)*

> *(Lights shift quickly from SETH to CAITLIN as
> SETH joins her. They are still talking on the
> phone until CAITLIN realizes SETH is standing
> right next to her.)*

CAITLIN

(Biting into the cookie.)
I'm not being dramatic: I am going to die. Either from stress or from Britney's never-ending death glare. Can you die from multiple things at once? I can *feel* her laser eyes *piercing* the back of my skull. I can't remember all those lines! I'm going to bomb and everyone is going to hate me!

(Pauses, takes a breath, she is feeling somewhat better now.)

The cookie actually really helped. Thanks.

(Some STUDENTS pop in.)

STUDENTS

(Sing-songy, with jazz hands.)
Snacks usually do that!

(STUDENTS pop out.)

SETH

You've totally got this.

(The lights shift from just CAITLIN to a wash of the stage. SETH, HARLOW, LEVI, SCOTTY, NORA, TEAGAN, OLIVIA, JACOB, STUDENTS all sit onstage to one side in profile towards MS. MAE, who stands addressing them from the other side. BRITNEY is also there, but in the back of the group. CAITLIN joins them all - she is the most visible. SM helps MS. MAE finish handing out scripts. The first page should say "The Winter Play" printed across it.)

MS. MAE
As we start, does anyone have any questions?

ASM
Of course Caitlin had a lot of questions, but mainly:

CAITLIN
(To herself.)
Why would you do this to me?

BRITNEY
(Raises her hand and then just stands up.)
Yes. Can I ask why you cast the show the way you did?

> *(Almost in unison, EVERYONE looks up from
> the scripts they just received to look at MS.
> MAE. They are very aware who spoke, but no
> one is willing to acknowledge BRITNEY.
> CAITLIN is staring at the front of her script
> where her name is written largely in Sharpie.
> She underlines it several times with a pen.)*

LEVI
(Stands up quickly and begins speaking.)
Look, everyone. I've been in five shows with Mae. Don't
question the process, she knows what she's doing. There are
no small parts, only small...

MS. MAE
(Raises her hand.)
Thank you, Levi, I appreciate the support, I do.
In a way, you're absolutely right. Each role *is* important to
the story we are trying to tell here. I know that it's kind of
like a behind-the-scenes tradition to cast the show amongst
yourselves before auditions - how you think it should be.
(Pauses, takes a deep breath.) But that always, always leads

18

MS. MAE (cont)

to someone getting upset. Every time, I tell you not to do it, but…

(MS. MAE's speaking turns unintelligible and shifts to the background as ASM speaks.)

ASM

Caitlin zoned out. She had heard this speech during the spring musical last year. Slipping her water bottle out of her bag, she took several large sips of water. As she was about to swallow, the unthinkable happened:

MS. MAE

…what do you think, Caitlin?

SM

The water caught in her throat and she felt all the blood in her body, maybe the world, rush to her cheeks.

(Coughing, CAITLIN stands up, trying to smile as water drips sideways out of her mouth down the front of her shirt. She tries to brush off the water. She gives everyone a nervous wave with both hands. During this, SETH makes an unsuccessful effort to pull her back down.)

CAITLIN

Um, sure. I'll say a few words.

(MS. MAE looks confused at CAITLIN's answer, but goes with it.)

ASM

Caitlin didn't know what words to say. She looked down at her shoes. One of the laces had come untied at some point, probably when she was cleaning off the vomit earlier. She made a mental note to wash them off better when she got home.

> *(CAITLIN clears the remaining water from her throat and tries to gather her spiraling thoughts.)*

CAITLIN

I think - I know I'm happy to be here. I - uh - I'm not good in front of people usually. I didn't know if I was going to try out, even when I walked into auditions. I don't know why Mae thinks I can do this - she's literally crazy. *(Nervously laughs.)*

I've come to shows here for a long time - since like fifth grade maybe? None of them have been bad. Well, maybe the Shakespeare one with the aliens? That was super confusing. *(Nervous laugh. Getting back on track.)* I just know it's nice to be here and be included. I'm gunna do my best and work really hard and I hope you all do too so we can have a really good show. Thanks.

MS. MAE

Th-thank you Caitlin. That was really, yeah, that was inspiring. I was just asking if you thought we should take a little snack break real quick before actually starting the read-through.

CAITLIN

Oh. Uh, yeah. That seems like a good idea.

> *(CAITLIN gives an anxious thumbs up. The STUDENTS change the set quickly for the next*

scene around CAITLIN as she sits down on the couch. EVERYONE except CAITLIN, SM, and ASM disappear. The lighting shifts dramatically to reveal the next setting.)

ACT 1 / SCENE 5 - Saturday Morning

Location: Caitlin's Living Room

(ASM crosses center stage with a cardboard sign that says "Caitlin's House." CAITLIN sits on a couch or loveseat. CAITLIN'S DAD sits in a chair or at a table nearby with a laptop. There may be other things around to indicate it's a living room. CAITLIN has a highlighter in one hand and her script in the other.)

SM
(Holding a cardboard sign that says "Saturday Morning.")
It was now Saturday morning.

ASM
Caitlin had stayed up until one-thirty last night with her script, but she wanted to double triple check that she hadn't missed any lines. This was a huge responsibility and she didn't want to mess it up.

CAITLIN'S DAD
(Without turning around.)
Homework already? You usually wait 'til Sunday night.

SM
Caitlin could see the title of the article her dad was reading:

CAITLIN
(Straining to read the title, mutters to herself without CAITLIN'S DAD hearing.)
Astronomers Hypothesize Connection Between Solar Flares and Amalgamating Supermassive Binaries. What does that even *mean*?

ASM
As a pharmacist, he liked sciencey stuff, which was not a trait Caitlin had inherited.

CAITLIN'S DAD
Roger, Roger? Anybody home?

CAITLIN
Uhhh. Yeah. This - *is* homework.

SM
She was not ready to tell the truth.

CAITLIN
Just like totally random English stuff.

CAITLIN'S DAD
Oh nice, I loved English. What've they got you on right now?

CAITLIN
It's the, uh, play - like, theatre unit.

ASM
But maybe a half-truth would be enough.

CAITLIN'S DAD
Are they having you read in class or anything? I loved doing that. I can close my eyes and be transported back to when...

*(CAITLIN'S DAD swivels in his chair towards
her, ready to launch into a full on nostalgia-fest.)*

CAITLIN

Yeah, uh, reading.

SM

Caitlin felt sweaty suddenly.

CAITLIN

I'm gunna do this upstairs.

> *(CAITLIN quickly gets up and heads out of the
> room.)*

CAITLIN'S DAD

Okay, love you, honey!

> *(CAITLIN'S DAD turns back to his space news
> unfazed.)*

ASM

A narrow escape, but she made it safely to her room where
she could scour the script in peace.

CAITLIN

Close call.

ACT 1 / SCENE 6 - First Rehearsal
Location: The Stage

> *(LEVI is standing on stage with his script getting
> ready to work on the opening monologue of the
> play. MS. MAE steps up next to him to use the
> monologue to help the cast understand what the*

set will look like. A few STUDENTS join from offstage. SCOTTY still has a sling on in this scene.)

SM

Monday's rehearsal started off pretty well, except for the eighteen times Caitlin fell victim to Britney's laser eyes.

(BRITNEY glares at CAITLIN.)

MS. MAE

Let's look at Levi's monologue here at the start. It contains some clues to the layout of the town and can help us get a picture of what the set will need to look like. Tech crew - pay special attention here.

Here on the line "Every morning, I take a walk across this bridge" - we get a clear indication this is happening near a river or some kind of water. Then, where it says "You can see the whole town if you stand at the one and only intersection. To the right, you can see we have a little pharmacy on the corner…"

(MS. MAE continues to describe and indicate, either quieter or silently, in the background during ASM's lines.)

ASM

Ms. Mae continued to describe the town and where certain characters lived and worked, painting a picture of a very complicated set. The tech crew started to look concerned at the workload that lay ahead in the coming weeks.

SM

Then, with a mischievous grin, Ms. Mae said:

(SM mouths MS. MAE's following line as if she's
remembering it fondly.)

MS. MAE
But there's actually not going to be any set.

(The STUDENTS look confused.)

Which is the way the playwright intended the show to be - as
little distraction from the message of the show as possible.

ASM
The tech crew shifted uncomfortably. But Ms. Mae was good
at anticipating the vibe swaps of teenagers. They probably
taught that in teacher training college: *Youth Mood Swings
101.*

MS. MAE
But that doesn't mean our lovely techies won't have
anything to do! There will be props and light and sound,
which will help us, and the audience, imagine a whole town
here on stage.

(SM/SIENNA steps into the scene and does what
ASM indicates.)

ASM
The stage manager stood up and assured the techies that
everything would be cool. That she'd seen this type of thing
before.

SM/SIENNA
*(To STUDENTS, reassuring them. Now in the scene as
herself.)*
I've seen this type of thing before. No worries, guys.

ASM

It was maybe a stretch of the truth, but she oozed raw confidence and the techies believed her and worshiped her, for she was their queen.

STUDENTS

Our queen!

BRITNEY

So you stole roles from *seniors* and now the *techies* too?

> *(A few STUDENTS start to get up to get a little distance away from BRITNEY.)*

MS. MAE

(Taken aback.)
Excuse me?

BRITNEY

You heard me, you…

ASM

(Waving her arms, interrupts BRITNEY. There is a light shift to focus on ASM. EVERYONE, except for ASM, freezes in place during ASM's next line.)

For the sake of the children present in the audience today, we won't tell you exactly what Britney said next, but we can tell you that she called Ms. Mae a very, very bad word.

> *(EVERYONE unfreezes and gasps - they are shocked at BRITNEY's disrespect. It is chaos.)*

JACOB

It was Britney!

MS. MAE

(Automatically in damage control mode.)
Wow, okay. Let's take a quick, uh, fifteen minute snack
break. Everyone back here at 4:00 *(Closes her script and sets
it down.)* If anyone goes for coffee *[you could mention your
local coffee shop here.]*, I'd take an iced mocha.

ACT 1 / SCENE 7 - First Rehearsal, A Few Minutes Later

Location: The Stage

*(NOTE: Go all out in the comedic flashback
moments in this scene, they serve as a contrast
to the otherwise genuine, emotional scene.*

*MS. MAE is facing the audience on one side of
the stage in a pool of light. She is in the
bathroom washing her hands. She grabs a paper
towel and dries off slowly. Looking in the
"mirror," she sighs deeply. Maybe she does part
of a theatre warm-up that she's done so much it's
become subconscious. She lingers a moment
longer than needed, gathering the strength. She
tosses the paper towel off stage as she walks out
the "door."*

*BRITNEY has been sitting with crossed arms in
the dark on the edge of the opposite side of the
stage. MS. MAE walks across the stage and sits
a few feet away and then turns to her. MS. MAE
waits to see if BRITNEY will say anything first,
but she does not. It is tense.)*

MS. MAE
So I - so I'm a little surprised by you. Where is all this
coming from?

ASM
(Not well lit, just a voice in the shadows somewhere.)
Britney didn't know what to say. She continued staring at her
baby blue manicure ruined by chew marks on her left
thumbnail.

> *(MS. MAE closes her eyes and rubs them with
> her hands, exhaling slowly.)*

SM
(Also not well lit, just a voice in the shadows.)
Ms. Mae couldn't deny that Britney had worked hard the
past few semesters, earning major roles in all the shows of
the previous two years. This included a memorable turn in
Peter Pan as a very Scottish Captain Hook:

BRITNEY
*(Jumps into a spotlit flashback, immediately in an over-the-
top characterization of a very Scottish Captain Hook - the
contrast should be alarming. If she can wear an appropriate
hat and hook that quickly - more power to you.)*

"Smee, tha' crocodile would hae had me afore this,
but by a lucky chance it swallowed a clock
which goes *tick tick* inside it, and so afore
it can reach me, I hear the tick an' bolt."

> *(BRITNEY sits back at her original position.)*

SM
The crowd was in tears laughing. Ms. Mae had looked
forward to it every night.

BRITNEY

(Not looking up.)
I thought you liked me.

MS. MAE

(Genuine.)
Of course - of course I like you.

BRITNEY

I don't know *why* I didn't get The Lead.
She's the main character and I'm your best actor and I
deserve it.

MS. MAE

(Carefully.)
There's no doubt you're talented. And you work hard. *So*
hard. *(Pause.)* I really respect that about you. That's
sometimes maybe even more important than talent. But you
have plenty of that too!

BRITNEY

Then why?

SM

Mae chose her words carefully. A scene from an episode of
an old cowboy tv show flashed across her mind from years
ago as she was falling asleep on her grandma's couch. A
wagon filled with explosives being transported across rough
prairie terrain.

MS. MAE

Sometimes an actor can be incredible, but still not be right
for a role. Not to bring in anyone else, but just as an
example. So Levi is amazing, *(LEVI pops into the spotlight
where Captain Hook just was.)* we both know that, but I
wouldn't cast him as a Romeo. *(LEVI feigns shock, maybe
clutching pearls.)* No one would believe it. *(LEVI shrugs and*

MS. MAE (cont)
ad-libs agreement.) It wouldn't work. But he'd be a fantastic
Mercutio, *(LEVI strikes a tragic pose.)* or maybe The Nurse.
(LEVI agrees, perhaps striking another pose.)

*(MS. MAE and BRITNEY laugh in agreement.
LEVI spins around and gets into character as
MS. JANE AUSTEN TEXAS over the next line,
adding at least a cowboy hat, but maybe
something sparkly too.)*

ASM
Levi had introduced the world to his alter ego, Ms. Jane
Austen Texas, last year at the talent show to a standing
ovation and an extra sparkly encore.

LEVI
*(Striking a pose to deliver the line with drama in a thick
Texas accent. Perhaps a moment of music to accompany.)*
"That there person, be it fella or ma'am,
who ain't got no *pleasure* in a good book
must be downright *foolish*… y'all."

(LEVI disappears after a flourishing finish.)

BRITNEY
(Back in the moment, genuine.)
But I don't see how I'm not right for the role. How am I not
right for The Lead?"

MS. MAE
(Taking the necessary time.)
Please don't take this the wrong way. You are too powerful.
Your performances are large. You shine *bright*. But this
character doesn't shine bright. Not from the beginning. She
finds her light in the middle of the show.

MS. MAE (cont)

(Pause.)

You've already found yours *here.*

(Gestures out to the theatre space.)

In another theatre, with a different cast, maybe you'd be the right person.

(Turns to face BRITNEY.)

In a way, you've outgrown our stage.

ACT 1 / SCENE 8 - Corner Piece

Location: Caitlin's Bedroom, Caitlin's Living Room/Kitchen

(SM crosses center stage with a cardboard sign that says "Caitlin's House." CAITLIN sits in her bedroom with her paper script, rifling through the pages. It is apparent that a teenager lives in this room. The action described is mimed dramatically, with CAITLIN indicating items through her interaction with them. This should be crisp and clear, using the space well. It's your choice if the brownie is real or mimed.)

ASM

The stage manager, Sienna, *strongly* recommended everyone put their script into a binder so as not to lose any of the pages. Caitlin wasn't the type of person to just leave spare binders lying around her room, so she needed to go on *the hunt.*

*(STUDENTS are gathered in the darkness
behind the action, humming something like the
Pink Panther theme song or similarly heist-
adjacent.)*

SM

(In an old-timey noir narrator voice.)
Carefully opening the bedroom door, Caitlin peered into the
dark hallway beyond. It was quiet.

CAITLIN

Too quiet.

SM

(In an old-timey noir narrator voice.)
Her mom's office, the most likely locale to obtain a loose
binder, sat grinning at her all the way at the end.

>*(CAITLIN tip toes down the hallway, holding her
>fingers up like a gun, moving in and out of the
>shadows.)*

The floorboards betrayed her, much like the spicy curry
she'd had for dinner.

>*(A STUDENT makes a squeaky floorboard
>sound. CAITLIN freezes, looks around, and then
>proceeds.)*

ASM

(In an old-timey noir narrator voice.)
But worry, she did not. Not a soul stirred. She traversed the
length of the endless hallway and breached the yawning
mouth of the deserted office. Moonlight freckled in through
the blinds across stacks and stacks of manila folders on the
glass-topped desk amid a graveyard of drained coffee cups,
the evidence of an overworked dame.

CAITLIN

(Breaking the noir vibe, as if talking into a walkie talkie.)
Pshhhht. Target in sight. *(To herself in her best* The
Godfather *accent.)* They don't call me Gutierrez the Ghost
for nothin'!

> *(OPTIONAL: As each of the slides go by on the
> "laptop" that CAITLIN is looking at, the
> STUDENTS recreate the scenes described in
> each photo. STUDENTS should include
> CAITLIN in the Nativity play "photo.")*

ASM

(Normal voice.)
The laptop screensaver blasted embarrassing photos of her
family vacationing at Arches National Park, going on their
annual sledding trip to the mountain, and volunteering at the
food bank on Thanksgiving. She stopped when the photo
flipped to an image of her when she was like four, wearing a
white oversized gown and holding a giant gold cardboard
star. Her grandma had put her in a Nativity play, which was
strange, because none of her family even went to church.

> *(CAITLIN shakes off the STUDENTS from
> around her in the "photo" like she's emerging
> from a thought. STUDENTS retreat to the
> background where they continue the humming,
> maybe a fresh song choice here more along the
> lines of the* Mission Impossible *or* James Bond
> *theme song.)*

SM
With no luck in the cluttered death trap of an office,
*(CAITLIN emerges through a "doorway" as if she's just
escaped with her life.)* Caitlin steered through the kitchen on
the way to the garage. She remembered her stuff from
middle school had been dumped into a box several summers
back and there just might be a binder there.

CAITLIN'S MOM
(From the couch with her phone and more stacks of papers.)
Midnight snack?

> *(STUDENTS hush each other. CAITLIN freezes
> halfway across the kitchen, tempted to duck
> behind the island. She hadn't seen the light on in
> the living room.)*

CAITLIN
(To herself, grimacing.)
Sooo *awkward.*

STUDENTS
(Whispering in unison.)
Sooo *awkwarddd.*

CAITLIN'S MOM
I think there's a brownie left. Just texting with your auntie.
She's having another crisis.

CAITLIN
Oh. Yeah?

ASM
She didn't know what to say, her aunt was a little scary.

STUDENTS

(Whispering in unison.)
Scaryyyy.

ASM

She was always trying to slather makeup on Caitlin.

STUDENTS

(Whispering in unison.)
Boooo.

> *(CAITLIN lifts up the foil of the brownie pan on
> the kitchen island and snatches the last piece.)*

CAITLIN

What is it *now*?

> *(CAITLIN chomps into the brownie.)*

CAITLIN'S MOM

Just a relationship thing.

STUDENTS

(Whispering in semi-unison, quieter, the joke is dead.)
Relationship thinggg.

CAITLIN'S MOM

Trying to help her through it.

CAITLIN

That's nice of you-u.

> *(A few too many crumbs spit out on the last
> word. CAITLIN needs milk.)*

CAITLIN'S MOM

You're up late, everything okay?

CAITLIN

School project-t?

SM

It wasn't technically a lie, just enough information to hold off the parental questioning.

CAITLIN

Needa binder, gunna grab from the garage.

CAITLIN'S MOM

Okay, don't stay up too late. Love you!

CAITLIN

(Swallowing hard.)
Good brownie.

STUDENTS

(Whispering in unison.)
Good brownieeee.

ACT 1 / SCENE 9 - An Iced Mocha
Location: Performing Arts Hallway

(BRITNEY stands in profile to one side of the stage. She is preparing to go in the theatre door. She wipes her sweaty hands on her shirt nervously. A blue binder is pinned between her arm and side. She holds a tray with two coffee cups [preferably from your local coffee shop], one should be an iced mocha.)

BRITNEY

(As she turns her phone on to "record" herself, her expression changes from hurt and sad to a performative, disrespectful sass.)
Britney here.
Sooo… Ms. Mae said I shine too bright for this play.
How is that even a bad thing?
Guess I'll shine *bright* as *The Love Interest's Mother*.

> *(BRITNEY sticks out her tongue at the phone, or something else to show displeasure. As she stops "recording" and puts away her phone, her face slips back to being hurt. She takes a sip of the one that is not an iced mocha and puts it back in the tray. She sighs deeply. She builds up the strength to face everyone and opens the door and enters. A group of STUDENTS are on stage talking.)*

STUDENT 1

Did you hear?

STUDENT 2

Did I hear? What did you hear?

STUDENT 1

I heard Britney say that -

STUDENT 2

- Ms. Mae said that -

STUDENT 3

(To BRITNEY.)
Did you hear?

> *(STUDENT 3 realizes who they just spoke to and veers in another direction. STUDENTS 1 and 2*

see BRITNEY and disperse. A fluid transition into the next scene.)

<u>ACT 1 / SCENE 10 - Happenchance</u>
Location: The Stage

(MS. MAE takes a long final slurp of her iced mocha and sets it down on the stage or a nearby stool. She stands still for a moment, positioned in front of the cast who are gathering onstage in the same formation as the script read-through. SETH and HARLOW don't need to be in this scene as they are onstage immediately in the following scene. SCOTTY still has a sling on in this scene.)

MS. MAE

Good to see you. Glad you're here. Hopefully you've taken some time to get to know your characters a bit and maybe, maybe the show too? We'll start where we left off yesterday. Any questions before we start? I'm excited for us to get going again.

(No one says anything. LEVI clears his throat in an elongated way, trying to fill the silence. CAITLIN shifts awkwardly. MS. MAE, again sensing the mood, takes it upon herself to break the tension.)

MS. MAE

Okay, so maybe I should address our weirdness from yesterday. I've chatted with everyone involved and we are, uh, on the same page. I believe in second chances. A second chance is happening right now. A little early in the process to use one, but so be it.

(MS. MAE smiles, she is hurt, but moving on. She scans the cast, meeting eyes but intentionally not lingering too long on anyone in particular. A few STUDENTS threw quick looks to BRITNEY, but she sits still, staring ahead, a stoic expression on her face.)

MS. MAE

Let's get on stage, yeah?

ACT 1 / SCENE 11 - Stapler
Location: The Ticket Booth

(On a front corner of the stage, SETH sets down a clear plastic bin. He carefully pops off the cracked lid, secured with a patchwork of duct tape. He begins pulling out branded shirts [perhaps ones that your theatre already uses]. HARLOW is going through a binder, or something else house management related. SCOTTY still has a sling on in this scene.)

SM

Seth neatly folded stacks of theatre t-shirts onto the concrete floor of the ticket booth where he and Harlow spent their afternoons tackling house management tasks.

SETH

(Checking tags as he goes.)
Three of these left. There's no mediums left of this style. And only a couple of the XLs.

(HARLOW nods, writing down the numbers of each as SETH dictates.)

HARLOW

I think we need to order a few more of the larger sizes. And kids' sizes. We don't have any left.

SETH

Good call. And some more stickers. Oof, I'm already tired. *(Collapses.)* I always forget how much work doing a show is.

HARLOW

You're not wrong. Will you type this up and send it to Ms. Mae, Seth, my dear? I will put these back where you got 'em.

SETH

Sure thang, chicken wang!

> *(SETH cackles. HARLOW raises an eyebrow. SETH snorts as he throws the shirts back into the plastic bin.)*

HARLOW

This is you on day one of the job?

SETH

This is me every day of the job! *(Laughs a little mischievously. Then, in a surfer dude accent.)* Tech is life, don't you know?

> *(HARLOW carries the bin of shirts across the stage. HARLOW knocks into SCOTTY part way across stage and fumbles with the bin until it hits the floor. This should feel like a "meet cute.")*

SCOTTY

Hey! Sorry! I was coming back to see you House Manger people. Ms. Mae said you have markers back there.

(Points to the corner where HARLOW just came from.)

I was supposed to highlight this apparently? This is my first play, I have no idea what I'm doing. *(Laughs.)*

(SCOTTY picks up most of his loose script from the floor, missing several pages after the collision, and helps put any stray t-shirts back in the bin, which he then lifts up and hands to HARLOW.)

HARLOW

Thanks, yeah, we have tons of highlighters! *(Picks up the several missing pages of SCOTTY's script.)* And we have a stapler if you need it too.

SCOTTY

Seems like you've got everything I've been looking for. *(Realizes this sounds intense. Awkwardly waves as he leaves.)* Uh. Thanks. Thank you.

ACT 1 / SCENE 12 - Invisible Cow
Location: The Stage

(Rehearsal is underway. TEAGAN and OLIVIA are in character, running through a scene while MS. MAE directs, perhaps from right off stage or maybe sitting in the front row of the audience.)

TEAGAN

(Onstage as THE MILKMAN, with an extremely poor Southern accent. Leading an invisible cow pulling a cart full of dairy products.)

"Come on, yuh old cow!
Ain't no time to die on me now.
Well, looky here. It's the scientist."

OLIVIA

(Onstage as THE SCIENTIST, with an equally uncomfortable German accent.)

"Vell hello! Miracle uff a day, issn't it?
How about zose klouds, yeah?"

TEAGAN

(As THE MILKMAN, slipping into a Minnesota accent.)

"Goshdarn clouds'll be gone by noon so much as I figure."

> *(Pulls an imaginary rope attached to the imaginary cow.)*

OLIVIA

(As THE SCIENTIST, still in an uncomfortable German accent. To the cow.)

"Hello zere, old kow. I didn't see you zere."

TEAGAN

(As THE MILKMAN, slipping into the worst possible Italian accent.)

"Woulda you alikea to buya some cheeze? You likea ze mozzarella?"

MS. MAE
(Ashamed of what is happening in front of her.)
Pause.

(Holds a finger in the air.)

Um. Please. Thank you. Yeah. Okay, good job everyone.

*(Gets on stage at some point during this. She is
holding a purple script notebook, she might have
a fun mug with some tea too.)*

First off. I appreciate the effort and the, uh, idea. Let's maybe
lose the accents. They are very, yeah, interesting, but not
really what we're *going* for here. Sorry. This doesn't take
place in the South. Or Minnesota. Or, um, *Italy*? Secondly,
none of those were really the actual lines.

JACOB
(Coming in from offstage or somewhere unexpected.)
Who's going to be the cow?? Can I be the cow? I'd like to be
the cow.

MS. MAE
*(MS. MAE, trying to hide a smile, sets her binder down.
Speaking to the STUDENTS and rest of the cast who are
trickling in from sides of the stage, sitting on the edge of the
stage, etc. This is a "teachable moment.")*
Okay, so we don't have a cow, true. Good observation,
Jacob. But we also don't need one. Just like we won't have
much *set* for this show, we also won't have everything
visually on stage that's supposed to be there either. So, the
cow is *there*, but not there. Olivia is essentially leading
around an *invisible* cow. For those of you in my classes, this
will be a good time to practice our miming skills we worked
on at the beginning of the year.

(JACOB sighs loudly, clearly disappointed he doesn't get to be the cow. There are several complaints about miming.)

BRITNEY
(She's the last to join.)
The audience has to read between the lines. Duh, you guys.

(She is clearly visible as she pushes through the crowd of STUDENTS.)

MS. MAE
Yes. *Thank you.* That's right, Britney.

ACT 1 / SCENE 13 - Ladder Scene
Location: The Stage

(Several ladders are standing open in the background. Two will work fine, but more and of various sizes could be good as well. NORA, TEAGAN, OLIVIA, JACOB and maybe a few STUDENTS are in the background among the ladders doing a theatre warm-up quietly, but they can be heard occasionally. CAITLIN is sitting cross-legged near the front of the stage going through her red script binder. She keeps slipping back and forth between several pages - she has forgotten to highlight an entire scene in the script. CAITLIN and SCOTTY are platonic pals, it shouldn't feel flirty at all. SCOTTY still has a sling on in this scene.)

CAITLIN
Oh no! What!?

SCOTTY

(Joins.)
Excited for the ladder thing?

CAITLIN

I didn't highlight this entire scene. What a disaster!

SCOTTY

It's okay, I got you. Harlow set me up with a solid collection
of these. *(Hands CAITLIN a highlighter.)*

CAITLIN

Thanks. Don't know how I missed it. Musta been tired.

> *(SCOTTY shrugs, flipping through his script,
> every page plastered with color. Holds it up to
> show CAITLIN.)*

SCOTTY

I think I have the opposite problem. *(Laughs.)* Want to run
through it while we wait for Mae to get back?

CAITLIN

Sure, yeah. *(Pause.)* I'm - the - ladders are freaking me *out*.

> *(SCOTTY chuckles and shuts his script, which is
> held together with a row of smiley face stickers
> and at least forty staples.)*

SCOTTY

Ah bro. Not my thing either, but we'll both be up there. Just
keep an eye on me and if you think you're falling, I'll make
sure I fall first. Then you can land on top of me!

CAITLIN

(Laughs.)
That's stupid, but I appreciate it.

> *(SCOTTY hops up and reaches out his hand to help CAITLIN up. She doesn't realize until she's already up, feels awkward, and gives him a high five on his outstretched hand.)*

Thanks, buddy.

ACT 1 / SCENE 14 - Gummy Bears
Location: Anywhere

> *(CAITLIN and SETH are sitting in a corner eating their lunch.)*

SETH

How are your lines going?

> *(SETH takes a substantial bite of yogurt or applesauce. CAITLIN caves to an impulse and shoves too many gummy bears into her mouth.)*

CAITLIN

(Almost drooling.)
I'b neber had to 'member so much schtuff in my li - my life.

SETH

That's beautiful. That should be your look for prom. *Attractive.*

CAITLIN

Shut the eck up, bub!

> *(She smiles as best as she can.)*

No ids like so tuff -

SETH

Maybe finish the gummy massacre first.

(Hands her his napkin.)

This is *atrocious* to witness.

(CAITLIN manages to pocket the bears into one cheek so she can talk.)

CAITLIN

It's actually so tough.

(Gasps for air.)

It's so much to memorize.

SETH

Yeah, I bet. *(A Darth Vader impression.)* Come back to the tech side, we have so much fuuun and there's no lines to memorize! Caitlin, I am your -

(SEITH surrenders another napkin to CAITLIN as she's drooling.)

CAITLIN

I can't believe Ms. Mae is *trusting* me with all this. Like what if I screw up the lines on staaage? I don't wanna be the jerk who forgot! Just standing on stage like - uhhhhh? And I think Britney is going to murder me in my sleep.

(Takes a gulp of her drink and reaches for another part of her lunch.)

Ze stress be *keeling* me.

SETH
Seems like you're scared of a lot of things.

CAITLIN
Well, a lot of things are scary.

SETH
You were scared to audition, but you did it anyways. Look where that landed you!

CAITLIN
Yeah, look where that got me. I wish I could fast forward to where I know the lines already.

SETH
You can! Close your eyes.

CAITLIN
What? Okay. Don't steal my lunch, *thief.*

(CAITLIN closes her eyes.)

SETH
Imagine yourself standing on that stage. Don't freak out! Just, like, actually see yourself there. You look great in your costume. You know your lines.

CAITLIN
I know my lines.

SETH
You are going to do great.

CAITLIN
I know my lines.
I am going to do great.

SETH

You are!

CAITLIN

I can picture it!

SETH

It's just going to take some time. And I'll help you.

> *(SETH scooches closer to her and puts his head
> on her shoulder, they embrace in a mutual hug
> that goes on too long and CAITLIN struggles to
> escape. She loves it.)*

<u>ACT 1 / SCENE 15 - Stool Stooge</u>
Location: Backstage

> *(Several STUDENTS, in a choreographed way,
> stack mismatched wooden chairs or stools
> center stage and then exit. CAITLIN enters on
> one side of the stage with her side bag. SM/
> SIENNA heaves onstage the opposite way,
> carrying comically too many chairs or stools
> and sets them down in the pile onstage during
> her line. SM/SIENNA is fully in the scene as
> herself.)*

SM/SIENNA

Sorry, didn't realize anyone would be coming in here so
soon. I was digging through the furniture closet and didn't
hear the bell!

CAITLIN

(Smiling.)
It's all good. Bell didn't ring yet.

(Sets her bag on the ground next to the pile.)

Ms. Mae asked me to try on my costume for the final act, so I snuck out of class early.

SM/SIENNA

Oh a little sneaky sneaky. *(Smiles.)* Nice. I'm trying to decide which of these work best for the ice cream sundae scene. Stools, obviously, but which ones? Here.

> *(SM/SIENNA motions for CAITLIN to sit down next to her on a pair of stools in front of the stack. They try several funny different combinations, but settle on two tall ones that are similar in height.)*

CAITLIN

Maybe I can have the tallest one? Then I won't look like such a *shrimp* next to Scotty.

> *(They both laugh. SM/SIENNA nudges CAITLIN friendly in the ribs. Pause.)*

You're not as scary as I thought you'd be.

> *(CAITLIN looks down at her shoes.)*

SM/SIENNA

What! What do you mean?

CAITLIN

Like, last year when I did tech, I never talked to you, even though you were my *boss*. I was *intimidated. (Pauses.)* But you're not scary at all. I mean, you *can* be when you need to be. But - I just - you're not like some kinda feudal overlord. *(Does a bad British accent.)* Back to work, peasaannts! I need my turnips!

SM/SIENNA

(Laughs.)
Um, thanks? *(Grins.)* But I know what you mean.

CAITLIN

You've been the stage manager a *while*, yeah? Since you were a freshman? That's weird.

SM/SIENNA

Yeah, Ms. Mae knew me already. My brothers were in shows with her, my dad helped some on sets. When they did *Beauty and the Beast*, my mom helped with costumes. My oldest brother Ethan was Lumiere, the candlestick guy, so the fam got pretty invested. I was in probably, what, fourth grade? They needed someone to be the little footstool dog thing, but didn't have anyone small enough. My mom volunteered me, so I was in all the shows too! Does that make me a nepo baby?

> *(SM/SIENNA pulls out some colored tape and a Sharpie and starts labeling the undersides of the chosen stools.)*

CAITLIN

Hey, you said it, not me. *(Laughs.)* So you *started* in the footstool business and look where that got you, *top* stool wrangler!

> *(SM/SIENNA snorts.)*

SM/SIENNA

HA. You're right. Veteran stool *stooge.*

(The bell rings.)

CAITLIN

Oh shoot, my costume! Ms. Mae will *keel* me if I'm late to rehearsal.

SM/SIENNA

(Imitating CAITLIN's bad British accent.)
Go on! Git to it, mista!

ACT 1 / SCENE 16 - Gravy
Location: Math Classroom

(CAITLIN sits in what is clearly a math classroom created with the chairs/stools from the previous scene. STUDENTS sit around CAITLIN, but she is the focus. HARLOW and SCOTTY [still with a sling on] are among the STUDENTS. P.E. TEACHER sits at the front of class, absorbed in a sports magazine, clearly substitute teaching.)

ASM

(Sitting in the seat behind CAITLIN, turns out to the audience.)
Everything whizzed by at breakneck speed. Caitlin remembered…

CAITLIN

*(Speaking aloud, but it's just her thinking. No one
acknowledges her talking.)*
Seeing my name on the cast list.

STUDENTS

(In unison, pointing up.)
At the top of the cast list.

ASM

And…

CAITLIN

Picking up my script at the read-through.

STUDENTS

(In unison, pointing up.)
From the top of the script stack.

ASM

And…

CAITLIN

Now it's somehowww a month and a half later.

ASM

Winter break was *next* week.

STUDENTS

(Without looking up, sung to the tune of "Deck The Halls.")
Fa la la la la, la la la la.

CAITLIN

Some sort of time-wizardry is clearly afoot.

SCOTTY
(Tapping HARLOW's shoulder.)
Hey, Harlow.

HARLOW

(Turning.)
Uh, yeah?

SCOTTY
Do you have a highlighter?

HARLOW
Of course I do.

ASM
There *had* been Thanksgiving break.

CAITLIN
Which is the *worst* possible holiday. But I didn't mind not having to go to school.

ASM
She had felt a little homesick for rehearsal as she sat at the table with her family, pouring tremendous amounts of gravy over unbearably dry stuffing. There was something mysterious about being in a play that she was still figuring out, something that clung thick in the air. That stuck to her insides. Like gravy.

CAITLIN
(Now everyone can hear her.)
Mmm gravy.

PE TEACHER
Did you say something, Caitlin?

CAITLIN

Oh - Uh. Sorry. *(Giving a thumbs up.)* Great job substitute
teaching. Good work.

STUDENTS

(Without looking up, sung to the tune of "Deck The Halls.")
Fa la la la la, la la la LA!

ACT 1 / SCENE 17 - Highlighters
Location: The Ticket Booth

*(HARLOW sits at a corner of the stage working
on something related to house management,
cutting tickets maybe. This is the last scene
SCOTTY has a sling on.)*

SM

Halfway through the last rehearsal before winter break, it
finally struck Harlow as suspicious why Scotty continuously
"lost" highlighters and needed to "borrow the stapler" almost
every day.

HARLOW

(Throws their head back and lets a single laugh erupt.)
HA!

ASM

A freshman walking by the ticket booth looked back with an
expression that could only be described as severe concern. *(A
single STUDENT walks by, possibly with a large instrument
case as they were probably just at band practice.)*

SM

Contrary to Harlow's job requirements as House Manager,
they could *not* tolerate most people and avoided them at
great lengths.

CENTER

ASM

But the *most* tolerable those days was…

HARLOW

(Smiling.)
Scotty.

> *(SCOTTY joins HARLOW with his hand out and
> HARLOW hands him a stapler or highlighter.
> It's a cute moment.)*

ACT 1 / SCENE 18 - Winter Break Forever
> *Location: Caitlin's Room, Caitlin's Living Room/
> Kitchen*

> *(SM crosses center stage with a cardboard sign
> that says "Caitlin's House." ASM crosses
> closely behind with a cardboard sign that says
> "Winter Break." CAITLIN sits on her bed on
> one side of the stage with her script notebook
> and something to indicate she's been playing
> video games.)*

CAITLIN

(Narrating as she's typing in her phone.)
It's been *literal* eternity since I've seen you. Snowflake
emoji. Crying emoji.

SM

Seth was on a trip with his family, leaving her all alone for
most of winter break.

> *(Several STUDENTS chorus line in with jazz
> hands from either side.)*

STUDENTS

(Sing-songy.)
Caitlin - was - all - alone! So - alone - and - lonely!

(STUDENTS scramble out.)

SM

Her own family's annual sledding excursion only knocked one day off the calendar. And since then, she'd been lying in her room alternating between gaming and scripting. She had repainted one of her walls with stripes, but now it felt more like a prison than the fun clown aesthetic she was hoping for.

(Near the end of the previous dialogue, CAITLIN'S LITTLE BROTHER, who is wearing superhero pajamas, slowly rises up from behind CAITLIN's bed and snatches the script binder.)

CAITLIN'S LITTLE BROTHER

AH HA! What's this!??

CAITLIN

(Jumping up.)
What the heck, stop! How did you get in here!?

CAITLIN'S LITTLE BROTHER

What is it?

(Reading the front of the binder.)

What's "The Winter Play?"

(The next part of the scene requires some fight choreography between CAITLIN and CAITLIN'S LITTLE BROTHER. Do so with as much gusto and comedy a sibling brawl can have. If you'd like, several STUDENTS can come in and carry

*the siblings around as if they're fighting in front
of a green screen - not necessary, but could
make it extra ridiculous.)*

CAITLIN

Give it back, that's mine!

*(CAITLIN grabs the script back from CAITLIN'S
LITTLE BROTHER and he jumps on the bed
after it. CAITLIN makes to dash out of the
room.)*

SM

Caitlin's little brother bellowed with the authority of a god, a
very small god in superhero pajamas. He leapt from Caitlin's
bed and landed directly on top of her, latching onto her like a
parasitic backpack.

CAITLIN'S LITTLE BROTHER

BAHAHAHA!!

CAITLIN

Get off, you freak! Get the - stopp!

SM

*(Suddenly quieter and as if it's a nature documentary -
perhaps an Australian accent. The action unfolds in slow
motion, assisted by STUDENTS if desired.)*
Here we can observe the adolescent female, her territory
threatened by a small, but relentless predator. Notice how
she evades the onslaught with a series of dodge and tumble
techniques, millions of years of evolution aiding her survival
instinct. And here, an attempt at playing dead to lure in the
attacker. A moment to catch her breath, as she could be on
the defensive for quite some time. And he takes the bait,
immediately regretting it as the homo sapien youth clamps
her appendages roughly about the unsuspecting juvenile and

SM (cont)

slams him not once, but three times against the nearby ottoman. His body is now useless. She stands atop the scene of the fight, surveying the damage. Only a few of her mother's papers were scattered across the carpeted floor.

ASM

(Still in nature documentary mode.)
The theatre script safely in the victor's grasp, the rivals keep their distance, circling around each other as they slink back through the kitchen. In a desperate attempt to retreat back to the safety of her domestic habitat…

CAITLIN

(Grabs CAITLIN'S LITTLE BROTHER in a headlock and holds up the script binder.)
You tell *no one* about this or I will *keel* you. You got it, bud?

CAITLIN'S LITTLE BROTHER

(Choking, but being a little over dramatic about it.)
Got - got it.

(CAITLIN'S LITTLE BROTHER runs off.)

CAITLIN

(Back in her room, narrating as she's typing in her phone.)
SETH. Will you help me bury the body if I have to kill my little brother? Knife emoji. Skull emoji.

*(Several STUDENTS pop in from either side
with jazz hands.)*

STUDENTS

(Sing-songy.)
Seth'll help bury the body! Bury the body! Bury the body!

(Lights out.)

<u>**ACT 1 / SCENE 19 - New Year's Eve**</u>
Location: Sienna's House

> *(Lights should slowly reveal different parts of the full party as more characters are mentioned. The scene should be well organized so all the action is clear and specific as described in the narration. SM/SIENNA is fully in the scene as herself.)*

ASM

(Holding a cardboard sign that says "Sienna's House." To audience.)
Welcome to Sienna's house.

> *(She throws the cardboard sign behind her and holds up another sign that says "New Year's Eve!")*

This is the annual theatre New Year's Eve party.

> *(She throws the cardboard sign behind her. Now in the scene as herself, to CAITLIN and SETH, who enter together.)*

There is a strict "no sparkle, no entry" policy. Sorry, I don't make the rules.

> *(ASM aggressively adds some sparkly accessories to their ensemble.)*

CAITLIN

You're worse than my aunt!

> *(LEVI and SCOTTY start chanting CAITLIN's name as CAITLIN and SETH enter.)*

60

CAITLIN
(Thoroughly embarrassed.)
You guys, *stop*. You guys!

> *(SETH joins in on the chanting and LEVI levels
> up his own by getting into character as MS.
> JANE AUSTEN TEXAS, stealing various articles
> of festive clothing from whoever can't escape.
> STUDENTS make a quick appearance with
> boxes of board games.)*

ASM
(To audience.)
The freshman techies unearthed Sienna's stash of family
board games within the first twenty minutes of the party,
banished themselves to the basement, and weren't heard
from the rest of the night. But they were happy. And Sienna
brought them snacks.

STUDENTS
(Chanting as they exit.)
Queen Sienna! Queen Sienna! Queen Sienna!

> *(SM/SIENNA follows the STUDENTS offstage
> with several bags of chips, etc.)*

ASM
At one point there was a white elephant gift exchange.
Someone brought a live mouse as a gift and, of course, the
little guy escaped when *somebody* tried to pet it.

TEAGAN
But it's *so* cute!

ASM

Based on its trajectory, it probably joined the freshmen in the basement.

There was a lip sync competition, which Levi of course dominated with Scotty and Jacob as overly suggestive backup dancers. *(Can be acted out, or not.)*

As the pizza supply dwindled and the gingerbread houses lay in ruins, the night gradually fizzled out, leaving only a few people, who found themselves sitting on the roof outside Sienna's bedroom even though it was like twenty degrees out.

> *(A pause. LEVI, SM/SIENNA, CAITLIN, SETH, HARLOW, SCOTTY sit huddled together. Everyone has had the best time and nobody wants it to end.)*

LEVI

(Breaking the silence.)
That was so *fun*, Siennaaa!

> *(He lays back and tries to make a snow angel in the heavy frost settling onto the roof, but nearly spills his hot chocolate all over himself in the process.)*

SM/SIENNA

(Taking LEVI's hot chocolate from him so he doesn't spill.)
Good. Glad you liked it. Almost - *almost* as good as last year at your house.

LEVI

I dunno 'bout that. What'd you think, Caitlin? Did you come to the party last year? I can't remember.

CAITLIN

(Still nervous around the upperclassmen.)
I did! It was super fun. Way different being a freshman
techie and now being in a show with a kinda big part.

HARLOW

(In an old-timey radio announcer voice.)
You mean THE part. You're the hot lead, the goshdang
STAR of the show!

SCOTTY

Okay, that's enough hot cider for you. *(Takes HARLOW's
cup of cider and chugs it, crinkles up the cup, and tosses it
off "the roof.")*

HARLOW

(In an old-timey radio announcer voice.)
The goshdang STAR, dahling!

CAITLIN

Uh. Yeah. Yes. Thank you?

SETH

(Cuddling up to CAITLIN.)
Don't be so humble. You're doing an amazing job.

SM/SIENNA

(Stretching her legs.)
You really are, you know.

SCOTTY

I mean, I literally know nothing, I've never been in a show.
But you're seriously killing it.

LEVI

Where's Britney? She was here wasn't she?

(SM/SIENNA jabs him sharply in the ribs.)

SCOTTY
(Pauses.)
Yeah. So… Britney and I broke up. Like a week into break.

*(SCOTTY pulls up his socks to help compensate
for wearing shorts.)*

CAITLIN
Oh no, I'm sorry.

SCOTTY
*(SCOTTY pulls down the sleeves of his t-shirt and brings his
bare knees closer in towards his chest.)*
It's fine. We weren't really getting along. I kind of feel bad
though. I came in and made friends with all you theatre
people. That's her thing.

SM/SIENNA
(Gathers the most tact she can.)
She's had her time with us, with everyone. She burns
bridges. That's kind of her thing.

*(SCOTTY shivers and wraps his arms around his
knees. HARLOW scoots closer, laying their
cardigan over SCOTTY's legs.)*

HARLOW
(Normal voice, sincere.)
You're with us now.

*(A silence falls over the group. A moment passes
and then CAITLIN loudly zips up her jacket.)*

CAITLIN
It's SO cold, can we go in?? I think I'm going to die.

LEVI

Thank goodness! I didn't want to be the one to say it.

<u>ACT 1 / SCENE 20 - Crepe Conversion</u>
Location: The Ticket Booth

(HARLOW and SCOTTY sit at the corner of the
stage. HARLOW was working on a house
management project until SCOTTY joined to
"get a highlighter.")

HARLOW

(With the most sincere of expressions.)
Something you need to know about me is that I am *obsessed* with crepes. And I take that obsession very seriously. You should be prepared to consume a substantial amount of crepes.

SCOTTY

(Equally as serious.)
I *respect* that, although I'm more of a frozen waffle guy myself.

HARLOW

(Getting back to work.)
Don't worry, you will be converted.

SCOTTY

Well, okay then. I look forward to it. And, as always, a splendid day to you!

(SCOTTY bows dramatically and walks part way
out the door with a highlighter.)

HARLOW

(In a posh accent.)
No, a splendid day to *you*, sir! A pleasure, as usual, I presume.

SCOTTY

(In a worse posh accent.)
The pleasure is and always will be *all mine. (Asking permission to leave.)* If I may then?

HARLOW

You may, good sir.
(Calling after him.)

We've been rehearsing for months! Not *sure* why you need highlighters still…

ASM

Harlow knew exactly why Scotty still needed highlighters.

ACT 1 / SCENE 21 - The Poster
Location: The Stage

> *(A group of STUDENTS, including CAITLIN, SETH, HARLOW, are gathered around MS. MAE, who holds a stack of posters for* The Winter Play.*)*

MS. MAE

Let's give it up for Harlow and Seth who put together the show poster for us! *(Starts a round of applause.)* They took my super vague idea and really ran with it - I love the vintage vibes!

*(HARLOW reveals the poster design to
everyone. ASM, in the scene as herself, passes
them out to everyone.)*

CAITLIN
(Holding a poster to the side of the group with SETH.)
I'm freaked. This makes it a *litttttle* too real.

*(She stares at the poster and bites back a
hangnail.)*

Like whose genius idea was it to make my name *SO* large on
this stupid thing!?

SETH

(Smiles mischievously.)
It could have been me…

CAITLIN
As soon as the first poster goes up tomorrow, my parents will
know *everything*.

SM
It was a small town, getting smaller by the second.

SETH
So the jig is up or...?

(Pauses.)

You could just… *not* tell them and see what happens.

SM
Seth thrived on chaos. As long as it was other people's
chaos, not his own.

CAITLIN

They're not going to be angry or anything - they're just…
too supportive.

SM

A terrible problem to have. But Caitlin had, if she was being
honest, lied to her parents.

CAITLIN

I can only stretch out the *(Imitating her own voice.)* "I'm at
Seth's house" thing for so long.

SETH

I mean, you were at my house a couple of times…

SM

She had told herself it was improv practice when she had
also fabricated an afterschool job at the library.

CAITLIN

Tonight. *(Sighs loudly.)* I've gotta tell them…

CAITLIN/SM/ASM/SETH

(Turning to the audience in unison.)
The Truth.

      *(Perhaps a dramatic acapella music moment - a
      la STUDENTS? Lights out with a flourish.)*

<u>**ACT 2 / SCENE 1 - The Truth**</u>

Location: Caitlin's Living Room

(ASM crosses center stage with a cardboard sign that says "Caitlin's House." SM follows closely with a cardboard sign that says "The Moment of Truth." CAITLIN'S DAD and MOM sit on the living room couch. The usual stacks of folders and other lawyery stuff are pushed to one side, slightly downsized from previous scenes. CAITLIN stands with a blanket over her shoulders, her script binder hidden underneath.)

CAITLIN

I have something to tell you.

CAITLIN'S MOM

(Sits up a little straighter and pauses what she's working on.)
Oh no, what's up?

CAITLIN

Well, you know how I said I've been hanging out with Seth a lot... I don't know, it just sort of happened.

(CAITLIN starts pacing, trying to find the right words to say.)

CAITLIN'S DAD

What is it, honey? You can tell us anything.

CAITLIN

Well, I - do you remember when I threw up at school?

CAITLIN'S MOM

I didn't hear about that.

CAITLIN
Okay, yeah, I did. And it's been a couple of months and…

> *(CAITLIN'S MOM grabs CAITLIN'S DAD's hand.)*

And now I have this big responsibility. Everyone in town is going to know soon anyways…

CAITLIN'S DAD
Can you skip to the part where you tell us what happened?

> *(CAITLIN'S MOM is holding her face, clearly stressed and confused.)*

CAITLIN
I'm not sure I'm ready. All the late nights, everyone staring at me, the ladders - the ladders really freak me out. *(CAITLIN'S MOM looks up, confused.)* All the changes, you know, the costume changes are a lot. I have to wear tap shoes at one point.

CAITLIN'S DAD
Tap shoes? We're going to need some more information, Caitlin.

CAITLIN
(A pause.)
I'm - I'm in the school play.

> *(CAITLIN'S PARENTS are visibly relieved.)*

CAITLIN'S DAD
(To CAITLIN'S MOM.)
What did I tell you? Job at the library? *Fishy.*

ASM
And then she told them everything about the play. Her role.
Seth's job. Britney's freak out. Ms. Mae's stupidity for
trusting her with the lead role. Why she didn't tell them in
the first place. How she knew they'd be so, so absolutely on
board that it freaked her out and that she...

CAITLIN
...wanted to do it on my own.

CAITLIN'S DAD
(To CAITLIN'S MOM.)
What did I tell you? Job at the library? *Fishy.*

*(CAITLIN'S MOM reaches out a hand to
CAITLIN.)*

CAITLIN's MOM
We would, we - yeah. You're right, we would have been - we
are - really excited for you. I know we can get - *enthusiastic*
- when it comes to this kind of stuff.

CAITLIN'S DAD
I'm sorry you felt like you needed to hide it from us instead
of talking about what you needed - or didn't need, I guess.
(Smiles.)

CAITLIN
I - I know. I wanted to see if I *could* do it. *(Humbly, not
bragging.)* But you've - got to see me. I'm like, I realized
I'm not as horrendous as I thought. *(CAITLIN slips the
binder out from underneath the blanket.)*

CAITLIN'S MOM
I'm sure you're much better than just *not* horrendous. I'm
sure you're wonderful.

*(CAITLIN'S MOM looks misty eyed, a sight
CAITLIN isn't used to.)*

CAITLIN'S DAD

And we'll certainly see you. We'll be there every night. If
that's okay.

<u>ACT 2 / SCENE 2 - Tater Tots</u>
Location: Backstage

*(CAITLIN, SETH, HARLOW, and SCOTTY sit
eating lunch.)*

CAITLIN

It was easy. Almost *tooo* easy.

*(CAITLIN strokes her chin in an overly
suspicious manner and twirls an imaginary
mustache. SCOTTY laughs, continuing to eat
cafeteria tater tots drenched in ranch. He adds
hot sauce from a bottle in his backpack.)*

SCOTTY

Aren't supportive parentals *the* worst! Mine even showed up
when I was into synchronized swimming. *(Eats more tots.)* I
do wonder how they'll do with a play though.

*(HARLOW grabs a tater tot and eats it,
coughing at the fiery sauce.)*

HARLOW

That is so, so u-un-unecessarily gross.

*(HARLOW chugs the remaining half of an iced
tea, then reaches for another tot.)*

CAITLIN

(To SCOTTY.)
I'm sure they'll be fine. *(Teasing.)* They'll be so *proud* of
their little *baby boy.*

SETH

(Disappointed.)
I don't think my fam is even coming. They were like: "We're
gunna come watch you give out tickets?"

SCOTTY

You just need your name on the poster, man. That's what'll
get 'em here. Trust me.

> *(SCOTTY adds a little more hot sauce to the
> surviving tots and HARLOW backs away, finally
> defeated.)*

CAITLIN

Hey, I heard someone in math talking about a bonfire this
weekend. Did you guys hear that?

SCOTTY

Ah, yeah, I went to one of those last year and it got pretty
rowdy.

HARLOW

Not my style. I'd rather be tucked into bed with my kitties
watchin' a lil scary movie or something.

SCOTTY

How about we all make some crepes?

SETH

Ohhhh fancy!

CAITLIN

Crepe making slash *(Makes a slashing motion and sound.)* horror movie night!! Can we do this? Are we doing this!?

SETH

Yes!! I'm in.

HARLOW

I'm game, let's do it! I'll pick something extra spooky.

ACT 2 / SCENE 3 - Time Travel (Or Whatever)
Location: The Stage

> *(Rehearsal is happening in the background. All, or as many as possible, of the scenarios described in SM and ASM's narration should be incorporated into the rehearsal sequences happening onstage.)*

SM

The production slowly came together. Caitlin saw it all happen last year on tech crew, when she helped build *the world of the play*. But this time around, she felt more connected to it all.

ASM

She noticed the difference it made when the chairs in the kitchen scene were placed at a slight angle.

SM

The way shadows cast behind her and Scotty while they were up on the ladders felt almost as important as the words they were saying.

74

ASM

The picnic scene found its spark when Ms. Mae coached
them to turn *a bit more* towards each other as they held
hands for the first time.

SM

The ensemble rehearsed the opening and closing of
umbrellas during the rain scene until it felt like a dance.

CAITLIN

(CAITLIN is talking to herself.)
Ms. Mae was right, the show doesn't need much to tell the
story. The little things make all the difference.

> *(MS. MAE calls out and gets both the cast and
> crew to stop where they are onstage and sit
> down. Some students lean against the wall, get
> comfortable, etc.)*

MS. MAE

We haven't talked for a few weeks about theme.

> *(Several students groan, including JACOB, and
> MS. MAE holds up her hands to silence them.)*

I know this isn't English class, but Mrs. Latch would be
absolutely thrilled we're talking about this. I gave you an
assignment to figure out what you think the theme, or
themes, of the show are. Anyone have anything?

> *(A few hands raise, CYNTHIA's goes up slowly.
> MS. MAE points at CYNTHIA.)*

Yes, Cynthia.

CYNTHIA

(Stands up. Quietly.)
Hi. Okay. Well, when I think -

MS. MAE

Speak a little louder so we can all hear you. Thanks. Doing
great.

CYNTHIA

(A little louder.)
Sure. Okay, I spent some time analyzing the show and read
up a bit about the playwright and came to the conclusion that
the central theme is family. There's the main families in the
story, but also chosen family. *(Gesturing towards the actors.)*
You'd never expect it between the milkman, the scientist,
and the tennis player. So yeah.

MS. MAE

Good, yes. I can totally see that. Thank you. Okay, who else?
(SCOTTY raises his hand. MS. MAE points to him.) Scotty.
What've you got?

> *(SCOTTY stands up and coughs into the crook of
> his elbow. His usual confidence is lacking and
> he seems a little nervous.)*

SCOTTY

I guess I'd say… this is a play about… *time travel*. Or
whatever.

> *(A few STUDENTS snicker, but MS. MAE
> gestures for SCOTTY to go on. BRITNEY, who
> can be clearly seen, slides her hands over her
> eyes and slumps down a little.)*

SCOTTY

Okay, so, sure, maybe I'm wrong. But - the play starts at the beginning, before, like, anything can go wrong and Caitlin's character isn't even born yet. Life is totally boring. Then there's the present, where we *currently* are, and things start to *go off*. Caitlin's character gets a little overwhelmed growing up, but is doing okay. She falls in love with my character. And then the play *zooooms* forward, Caitlin's character is in the future after my character has died - sorry about that, guys - and we see her looking backwards wondering about stuff. Like, if things could have turned out any different if she'd made other choices and not murdered me. Totally on accident, of course! And all throughout, she's going back and keeping memories alive with the flashbacks. So… yeah. Time travel, guys.

MS. MAE

I like it, Scotty. I can safely say I've never thought of it that way. But it does make sense the way you describe it. So, we've got family and time travel. *(Sits down cross-legged on a chair and leans forward.)* Okay, who's next?

ACT 2 / SCENE 3 - The Last of Laser Eyes
Location: Backstage/The Dressing Room

SM

Britney understood that while she was a part of the play, it wasn't *her* show like previous productions. *(BRITNEY walks to and stands center stage.)* When she walked on stage during rehearsal, people didn't stop what they were doing to watch. And as she exited back into the wings of the stage, the mob of freshmen techies didn't part down the middle like they usually did. *(A crowd of STUDENTS rush by BRITNEY from one side of the stage to the other, she is caught in the middle of them and is overwhelmed.)*

BRITNEY

(Hissing.)
Excuse me. *Excuse* me!

> *(During SM's next line, a STUDENT from each side of stage wheels on a costume rack and positions them to either side of BRITNEY to create the dressing room. The costumes on the racks could be the ones used for* The Winter Play. *The STUDENTS who wheeled the racks, should stay with them through the scene - they are the costume assistants and can be doing some simple, smooth choreography with the racks in the background, all while listening in on BRITNEY.)*

BRITNEY

("Recording" on her phone.)
Britney here…
Sorry I haven't posted in awhile.

> *(Sad, angry, hurt.)*

I'm *so* embarrassed to be a stupid *side* character in this stupid play.
I have like *no* lines and no stage time.
I've worked *so* hard for years and I earned the spotlight.
But…

> *(Pause, a shift.)*

…after I graduate.
And go audition in the *real world*.
I know that…

> *(Stops "recording" and puts her phone down.)*

BRITNEY (cont)
I'll have to earn the spotlight again…

>*(Starts shaking her head, trying not to cry. She turns to exit the dressing room, but catches her reflection in the "mirror." She pauses for a moment to affix a more neutral expression. She dabs at her eyeliner, which has gotten a little smudged. Almost smiling, almost crying. BRITNEY doesn't notice the pair of STUDENT costume assistants in the dressing room until right now. As she lasers in on them, they dodge eye contact.)*

What? What are you looking at!?

>*(They are suddenly very interested in counting the hangers on the costume racks, which they quickly wheel away.)*

ACT 2 / SCENE 4 - Church
>*Location: Levi's Church*

>*(As the scene starts, ASM holds up a hand painted sign that says "Levi's Church" and then walks off. STUDENTS hold holiday garland and decorations in place to create a shape for the church lobby. STUDENTS hum a hymn softly in the background and LEVI'S MOM hums along somewhat poorly. LEVI straddles the top of a ladder as he reaches for some of the garland strung across an entrance to the church sanctuary. LEVI'S MOM grips the ladder below and feeds the out-of-season decorations into a*

*cardboard box. LEVI tosses a paper snowflake
and it flutters perfectly into a trash can nearby.
They continue the work throughout.)*

LEVI'S MOM

Careful, honey! *(Raises a hand to support him if he falls.)*

LEVI

I'm fi - ohh! *(He jerks to one side, pretending to lose his
balance. Laughs.)* I'm *fine*!

LEVI'S MOM

Levi!! *(Pointing up at him.)* Don't you dare. *(She is used to
his shenanigans.)*

LEVI

Okay, okayy. *(He makes a slight motion like he might do it
again, but doesn't when she gives him a look.)*

LEVI'S MOM

How's the play coming along? You've been working on your
lines so much.

LEVI

Lots of lines - probably the most I've ever had. Makes *The
Crucible* look easyyy.

LEVI'S MOM

Oh! You were so good in that! I cried every night. *(Pause.)*
I'm sorry your dad hasn't come to your shows. It's a shame.
I'll try to get him to this one.

LEVI

(Sad, but smiling.)
Thanks, mom. I know you'll like it. There's this one bit in the second act where I do that thing Uncle Sean always does with his arms. *(Does a unique arm gesture, laughs.)* I think that alone might make dad laugh.

LEVI'S MOM

I'll see what I can do, but you know how he gets.

LEVI

(Slightly sarcastic, but still with LEVI charm.)
Tell him that one of the leads is on the football team, maybe that'll get his attention.

LEVI'S MOM

Levi. You know he didn't mean it when he…

> *(LEVI's phone vibrates in his pocket. A STUDENT makes the vibrating noise and LEVI can show it by grabbing at his pocket several times. LEVI sits down on the top rung of the ladder to read a text. He looks concerned after a moment.)*

LEVI'S MOM

What is it?

LEVI

I've gotta go. Sorry, I'll be back in a bit to finish helping you.

LEVI'S MOM

Oh, okay. That's fine. Thanks for your help so far.

(LEVI slides down and gives his mom a quick hug.)

LEVI

Gotta give some silly kiddos a ride. You were right, the bonfire got a little wild.

<u>ACT 2 / SCENE 5 - Extra Extra</u>
Location: The Stage

(MS. MAE is at the front of the theatre. All cast and crew members of The Winter Play, *except LEVI, are trickling into the theatre through the aisles with their backpacks, instrument cases, etc. as if they are arriving after school and join together on the stage. SM/SIENNA and ASM, who are in the scene as themselves, enter from backstage, they have already heard the news.)*

MS. MAE

(Really tired, it's been a long day.)
We have some news. Yeah. Everyone take your seats and we'll get to it.

(She rubs her eyes as the cast and crew get settled.)

Okay, so I've just met with our principal, Mr. Simons, and he's given me some information. I'm sure some of this is already known since you all chat so much outside rehearsal. I'm only going to tell you so you have the facts and so some rumors can be put to rest. There was a bonfire down at the water on Saturday night. Who knows, maybe some of you were there. Doesn't really matter.

*(She takes a deep breath and looks up at the
ceiling for a moment.)*

MS. MAE (cont)
Levi and some other students were on their way home and,
well, they got pulled over. Long story short, a couple of the
students had some illegal items, um, loose in the car. From
my understanding, Levi didn't know this at the time, I
assume he was trying to get everyone home safely. Who
knows, not my - *our* job to figure it out. But he's being held
responsible since it was his car.

(Pause.)

Um, yeah, school rules are not entirely clear on something
like this, but what we do know is that Levi is being pulled
from after school activities until everything is figured out.

(There is absolute silence.)

Any questions?

(Lots of hands shoot up.)

Okay, yes, Nora.

(Points to NORA.)

NORA
So - what - I'm sorry, I just transferred here. I'm confused.
What does that mean?

MS. MAE
That means he will be at school, but not joining us for
rehearsals this week. Or tech rehearsals next week, and…
probably the performances the next weekend.

                    (STUDENTS respond, talking amongst
                    themselves.)

                         MS. MAE (cont)
Yes, Sienna.

                         SM/SIENNA
But we *are* still doing the show, yeah? And if so, who will
play The Narrator instead of Levi?

                            ASM
(A side comment to the audience.)
That's a biggg role.

                          MS. MAE
Yes. Good questions. We are still doing the show. We have
time to pull this together. I have some initial thoughts about
recasting, but I need to talk to a few people first. I will let
you all know by the end of rehearsal today. Who else has a
question - yes, Olivia.

                           OLIVIA
Did Levi get arrested?

                          MS. MAE
That is something I don't know, nor is it my business. Not
really any of our business. But this *show* is our business and
so that's what we can focus on right now. Yes, uh. Yes,
Jacob.

                           JACOB
Uh, how many drugs did Levi smoke? Ha.

                    *(JACOB is the only one who laughs. MS. MAE
                    inhales and blinks slowly.)*

MS. MAE

Okay, so any *other* questions about how this will impact the
show? If not, I'm going to talk to a few people. Let's start
rehearsal in like fifteen? We'll meet back here then.

ACT 2 / SCENE 6 - The Mutant
Location: The Stage

> *(EVERYONE is in similar positions as they were
> in the previous scene. HARLOW and SETH
> make their entrance through the crowd on
> SETH's lines. MS. MAE enters, carrying a stack
> of her rehearsal paperwork, which she sets on a
> stool. SM/SIENNA and ASM are in the scene as
> themselves.)*

MS. MAE

I've chatted with a couple people and I think we've come up
with a good plan. *(Pause.)* To replace Levi, I have invited
our friend Britney to take over the role of The Narrator. She
works hard and was around when we had to replace some
fairies in *Midsummer* two years ago. She's got what it takes
to pull this off. Yes, Jacob, I see you have a question. Let me
finish and I'll take it.

JACOB

(Does not let MS. MAE finish.) How'll Britney do two roles?
They're onstage at the *same* time. Is she gonna change
costumes real quick or something?

MS. MAE

(With a very long blink and the utmost patience.)
Like I said, I'll take questions after this. But let's take a
minute to acknowledge the amount of work Britney has
ahead of her, and maybe we can think of the best ways to

MS. MAE (cont)

help her get there. Along with that, since Cynthia has done such a great job so far with this show, *(Indicates CYNTHIA. CYNTHIA waves.)* I've asked her to take over Britney's old role as The Love Interest's Mother. That will also be a lot of work. Thank you both for stepping up and agreeing to make this big commitment for us. We'll all do what we can to help you.

> *(ASM leads a round of applause or snapping. SM/SIENNA is scratching out and rewriting names on the cast list she carries in her production notebook.)*

SM/SIENNA

That means The Newspaper Boy needs to be replaced by someone too.

MS. MAE

(Nodding.)
That's true, thank you, Sienna.

> *(A pause and then SETH clears his throat near the back of the theatre.)*

SETH

Um, I'll do it.

> *(CAITLIN turns, recognizing SETH's voice. EVERYONE else turns a few seconds later. CAITLIN laughs, not understanding.)*

JACOB

You're a techie though. Can he even do that?

CAITLIN

Seth! Are you serious? *(Throws up her hands.)*

HARLOW
(Jokingly, but also a little serious.)
Please, pleaseee take him away from me!

SETH
Yeah! Why not? Being a techkid means doing what's gotta
be done. I'll take one for the team.

HARLOW
*(Walking up the aisle next to SETH, smiles mischievously
and tries to get a chant started.)*
Tech can act. Tech can act. Tech can act!

> *(SCOTTY joins in, then CAITLIN, and then
> EVERYONE. It is a triumphant moment and
> SETH is the star. CYNTHIA and BRITNEY get
> centered in the celebration as well. MS. MAE
> allows the moment to get out of hand, standing
> back, but joining in the chant.)*

ACT 2 / SCENE 7 - Recycling
Location: Ms. Mae's Apartment

> *(ASM stands center stage with a cardboard sign
> that says "Later That Night" and then adds an
> additional, smaller sign that says "The Theatre
> Teacher's Home." The large "murder board" is
> in the background. ASM adds the signs to a pile
> of cardboard recycling next to a sitting chair,
> revealing MS. MAE standing center stage in
> pajamas and a purple bathrobe. She holds up a
> wine glass and dramatically pours a very full
> glass of chocolate milk, which she then takes*

with her as she steps daringly over the large
recycling pile to sit on the chair.)

SM

Ms. Mae poured herself a glass of chocolate milk and brought the carton with her. She stepped around the pile of overflowing recycling and sat on her favorite chair in her over-priced two-bedroom apartment. Across the highway from the high school, she lived just far enough away that she rarely saw students at the grocery store, but it was still a constant concern. She often shopped late at night to avoid any unnecessary awkward encounters.

ASM

It wasn't that she didn't love her students, she just needed some personal space.

SM

(To ASM, sitting on one of the chair arms.)
That seems reasonable.

ASM

(To SM, sitting on the other chair arm.)
I think so too.

SM

She took a long sip and set the glass down next to a stack of short stories she had failed to grade again. Harlow, the semester's stand out Creative Writing student, would give her hell again. Hopefully they'd understand though, given the *circumstances*.

MS. MAE

(Lifting up a few of the short stories.)
I really should convert to digital. Less recycling.

ASM

It wasn't the first time Ms. Mae had to recast the show at the last minute.

SM

It didn't usually happen that late, but in the end, all she could do was move forward as efficiently as possible.

ASM
(Excited, but nervous. To SM.)
Oh my gosh, opening night is only like two weeks away!

SM

(To ASM.)
Don't remind me!

(To the audience.)
In this case, at least, Ms. Mae didn't have to *ask* a student to leave a show because of a bad attitude or lack of effort. She remembered saying…

MS. MAE
(Sitting forward and drifting back to the moment in her mind.)
It's not personal, I *promise*.

SM

…to my brother, Ethan, six years ago.

MS. MAE
(To the imagined Ethan.)
It's just not working out this time. Maybe let's try again with the spring musical?

SM

He had been consistently late to rehearsal and failed to memorize his lines *well* past the memorization date. So it was probably a good call on her part.

MS. MAE

I should take the recycling out.

ASM

She knew full well she wouldn't take the recycling out for another two weeks when the show was finally over. That's just kinda the way it was.

ACT 2 / SCENE 8 - The Newspaper Boy
Location: Anywhere

> *(A crowd of STUDENTS walks across the stage with backpacks and lunch bags/trays, heading to their lunch break [perhaps taking off the set pieces from the previous scene]. CAITLIN and SETH are sitting in a corner going over lines.)*

CAITLIN

How are your lines going?

> *(CAITLIN smirks at SETH. He lays stomach-down on the floor next to her with his newly highlighted script. CAITLIN reads his script upside down in a terrible Minnesota accent.)*

"Extry! Extry! Read all aboot it!
Snow blizzard o' the century 'bout to hit he-ya!"

(They both gag with laughter. SETH snorts into his script.)

SETH

Ahh! Maybe *you* should be The Newspaper Boy. No, actually it's not that bad. It's like twelve lines. I'll have it by rehearsal. *(Threatening.)* Or I'll *quit.*

CAITLIN

Nooo, don't quit! Here, stand up.

(They both stand up. CAITLIN helps position SETH.)

Okay, so this is the audience *(Indicating the audience.)* and you're here.

(Forcing him to turn at a slight angle to the audience, but he doesn't comply.)

Don't face the audience straight on, that's creepy and looks weird. Just pretend like no one's there.

SETH

Well, no one's there. *(Indicating the audience.)*

CAITLIN

No, I know. But pretend you're on stage and that's the audience. *(Indicating the audience.)*

SETH

Okay, that's the audience. *(Half-heartedly indicating the audience.)*

CAITLIN

Exactly. That's the audience. This is you.

(Grabbing his shoulders and getting him to turn a bit.)

CAITLIN (cont)

Now do the line.

SETH

(Way too quietly.)

"Extra. Extra. Read all about it…"

CAITLIN

What did you say?

SETH

(Barely louder.)

"Extra. Extra. Read all about…"

CAITLIN

(Cupping her hand to her ear.
What was that??

SETH

(A little louder.)

"Extra. Extra. Read all…"

CAITLIN

SAY IT AGAIN LIKE YOU MEAN IT!

SETH

(A little too loud.)

"Extra! Extra! Read all about it!
Snow blizzard of the century about to hit!"

CAITLIN

(Salutes him dramatically.)
There you go, captain. That's it. That's what we're looking for.

(Gives SETH a really hard high five.)

SETH

(Nodding.)
Okay, Ms. Caitlin Gutierrez. I see you. Seems like somebody knows their stuff now, huh? You can make a tech kid into an actor!

CAITLIN

I've picked up a thing or two.

SETH

You think I can do this?

CAITLIN

You were born to play a little newspaper boy. You're going to be *so* cute!

SETH

Cute?

CAITLIN

Oh, sorry. *(In a deep voice.)* You're going to be SO *manly*! The manliest little newspaper boy there ever was! Get you a big beard and you'll be SO manlyyy.

SETH

I think I'll stick with cute.

CAITLIN

(Normal voice.)
Oh! But don't forget!

(Rummages around in her side bag. As an old wizard.)

CAITLIN (cont)

It's really ever so dangerrrousss to go all alonnne, this *he-ya* cookie will protect you!

(Hands SETH the same type of cookie he handed her in Act 1 / Scene 4.)

SETH

Thanks, wizard man!

CAITLIN

(Normal, but commanding voice.)
Okay, let's run your lines, techo! Chop chop! From the top!

ACT 2 / SCENE 9 - The Monarch
Location: Onstage, Backstage

SM

It was only a few days until opening night and the to-do list was never ending. As the stage manager, I was especially thankful the set was so minimal. In the past, the techies often worked on last minute details up until a few hours before the audience walked in and took their seats. It's realllly stressful.

ASM

For this show, the most complicated thing was the absolute jigsaw puzzle of random furniture to store and coordinate. Ms. Mae's vision was to have everything on stage at all times - sort of a cluttered pile at the back of the stage.

SM/SIENNA

While it might have looked like a chaotic heap to the audience, I wanted it precisely organized for the often *forgetful* actors. I created an elaborate system of colored and numbered tape on the floor that matched with tape on each piece of furniture.

(Now in the scene as herself.)

So this is an excellent job for you, my beautiful assistant stage manager. I'd like you to record the colors and numbers. And then draw a diagram of everything.

ASM

(Now in the scene as herself.)
U-um. You sure you want me to do this?

(Aside to the audience.)

I was new to theatre, but Ms. Mae had me in Creative Writing and recommended that I sign up for tech. It had all been a *little* overwhelming to get used to. Theatre kids are, as I told my dad after a few days of rehearsal: *"Different."*

SM/SIENNA

(In the scene as herself.)
Yes. You can totally do this. You did great writing up the blocking for Act Two. It's been super helpful and, most importantly, I can read your handwriting.

> *(Opens her overflowing, but neat, binder and pulls out several checklists. Now to the audience.)*

Time to circle back in with the freshmen I reluctantly released to "reorganize" the workshop.

SM/SIENNA (cont)
(Shaking her head.) I'll probably have to do it again myself.
Who am I kidding?

(Now in the scene as herself, to ASM.)

Okay, you good?

(Doesn't wait for ASM to respond.)

You're good. I'll be back in a few.

ASM
(Now to the audience.)
The freshmen techies in question were standing in a loose
circle around the workshop.

> *(SM/SIENNA walks across the stage and is met
> by STUDENTS doing what is described. It is
> spooky. An eerie sound underneath it all would
> be appropriate, perhaps some organ music or
> perhaps STUDENTS are humming.)*

It was like a still life painting, each of them in some sort of
trance holding something: a random chunk of a two-by-four,
a crusty paintbrush, a can of mismatched screws, a broom
being swept pathetically over the same spot over and over
again. One lost soul was standing at the paint cleaning sink,
the water running, just staring down the drain.

> *(SM/SIENNA, in the scene, claps and stomps
> several times to get the techies' attention.)*

SM/SIENNA
Y'all awake!? Where are we at? Have you done anything at
all yet?

STUDENTS
(In one fluid motion, all STUDENTS' heads turn to face their monarch.)
Sienna. Siennaaaaa.

SM/SIENNA
Uhhhh, *creepy* you guys.

(EVERYONE is frozen except for ASM.)

ASM
(To audience. Indicates who is who as she speaks.)
Every single one of these freshmen techies will sign up to help with at least the next three shows. This is their ultimate high school destiny. One of them will discover they like being *on* stage more than backstage and eventually get the lead role of Bert in *Mary Poppins* their senior year. One will get really into photography and take photos and headshots for several of the shows. Another will rise to replace Sienna as stage manager, a queen in her own right.

SM/SIENNA
(To audience.)
But that all seems impossible at the moment.

(Sighs. Now in the scene as herself.)

Okay, everyone. Let's do this together shall we?

ACT 2 / SCENE 10 - Mime O' Clock
Location: Backstage

(BRITNEY sits off to the side of the stage.)

SM

Harlow had made Britney a new copy of the script, even
adding three hole punches and putting it in a fresh binder
with a fun little cover. And Scotty spent all of math class
highlighting The Narrator's lines before handing it over.

*(SCOTTY walks up and hands BRITNEY the new
script.)*

SCOTTY

You've totally got this. You're always *so* good.

*(SCOTTY grabs BRITNEY's hand and gives it a
squeeze.)*

BRITNEY

Thanks, Scotty.

*(BRITNEY reveals a softer side of herself for a
brief second. They share a moment, maybe they
hug, and a lot is said in the silence before
SCOTTY exits.)*

ASM

It wasn't that Britney couldn't handle a lot of lines. Or that
she'd never had this many before.

BRITNEY

(To herself.)
Obviously.

SM

It was just the ridiculously short time frame she had to
memorize them all and…

BRITNEY

(To herself.)
…not look stupid in front of everyone after being a total
wreck for months.

ASM

This was an opportunity for penance, and she knew it. If she
could do this…

BRITNEY

(To herself.)
Maybe things could be patched up a bit and go back to -

(Several STUDENTS walk by.)

STUDENTS
- something resembling normal.

BRITNEY
(BRITNEY flips several pages in her binder. To herself.)
The lines, okay. I've totally got this. But the character is
something else.

ASM

She was nervous about filling Levi's shoes without
disappointing everyone. He was a legend and -

BRITNEY

(To herself.)
- just *so* good.

SM

He had crafted the character as a sort of speaking Charlie
Chaplin with a lot of miming, which shouldn't have worked,
but it did *because* it was Levi.

BRITNEY
(BRITNEY tries to do some Charlie Chaplin-like miming.)

"You can see the whole town if you
stand at the one and only intersection..."

> *(She tries the same unique Uncle Sean arm
> gesture LEVI does in Act 2 / Scene 4. To herself.)*

I don't think I can pull it off the same way.

ASM
She would need to go about the character from a totally
different angle. Her brain kicked up part of a line from her
giant monologue at the end of Act Two while she tried to
find the character.

BRITNEY
*(Taking on a tone and seriousness not yet seen from her, but
that will be shown in later scenes when she is in character
again.)*

"It's not the universe that asks us the question,
it's something we must ask of ourselves..."

ACT 2 / SCENE 11 - Opening Night, Behind The Curtain
Location: Backstage

> *(The preshow announcements crackle over the
> speakers recorded in SM's voice, perhaps what
> is usually used in your theatre: "Please silence
> your cellphones... no food or beverages in the
> theatre... small children are... etc." CAITLIN
> stands "backstage" waiting for her entrance
> cue. The "backstage" effect can be achieved by*

*having characters on extreme sides of the stage,
lit in specific lights, or positioning near the
curtain - it really depends on the structure of the
space being used. The important thing is that
characters are fully visible when "backstage."*

*CAITLIN is in costume as THE LEAD - an era-
appropriate outfit for a rural school. She adjusts
the waist of her outfit and shifts the stack of
books in her hands.)*

ASM

(To audience.)
After so many rehearsals, Caitlin knew where she needed to
be, but she still felt in the way. She was in the way in the
makeup hall while everyone got ready for the show. She was
in the way in the changing room, the green room. Backstage.
Everywhere.

*(CAITLIN stands back so BRITNEY can grab
the wooden chairs CAITLIN is blocking access
to. BRITNEY is in costume as THE NARRATOR
- a wooden pipe in her mouth and an era-
appropriate outfit for an older man, perhaps a
vest and a hat.)*

Always in the way.

SM

(To audience.)
Caitlin kept finding herself in a daze, suddenly super aware
of where she was, but no idea how she had gotten there.

*(CAITLIN looks around, a little confused how
she got there. The next sequence could be acted
out in the background in a way similar to the
witch at the beginning of the show.)*

SM

She pictured a time machine, smoke pouring out as the door swung open to some future land, the local apocalyptic warlords accepting her as their own before...

CAITLIN

(To herself.)
Maybe Scotty was right about the theme of the play.

ASM

(To audience.)
And now she was here and the audience - you guys *(Points throughout the audience.)* - was a few feet away from the curtain. Oh, look, it's Levi!

> *(LEVI should be in the front row of the audience.)*

SM

(To audience.)
Caitlin was thankful to not be the first character onstage. Her hands were sweating and it was too late to fix her makeup which she could tell was already starting to *go*. She could not remember her first line.

CAITLIN

(Panicking, speaking to no one.)
I can't remember my first line. It's something about... being good at memorization.

ASM

(To audience.)
That's a bit of a stretch. And the next line, fourteen pages in the script later, was something like...

CAITLIN

Something like… Yeah, I can't remember.

ASM

Fortunately, in all the turmoil around Levi's absence, Ms. Mae had cut a tiny, tiny bit of slack with line accuracy. What was it she'd said?

MS. MAE

(Appearing.)
You know the story.

MS. MAE and CAITLIN

Tell the story.

(MS. MAE disappears.)

CAITLIN

I am going to suck and Ms. Mae will hate me and so will everyone else. I *am* going to forget my lines.

SM

(To CAITLIN, passing next to her.)
You're going to remember your lines. You're going to do great.

CAITLIN

(Convincing herself.)
I am going to remember my lines.
I'm going to do great.

ASM

(To CAITLIN, passing next to her.)
Break a leg, Caitlin.

CAITLIN

I am going to remember my lines.
I am going to do great.
I am going to break my leg.

> *(She continues to repeat, but quieter.
> STUDENTS, from offstage or peaking on, join
> her chant with "break your leg.")*

SM

(To audience.)
Caitlin repeated this over and over again until it was the only
thing she could think...

ASM

(To audience.)
And the only thing that was true.

> *(Chant stops. BRITNEY walks past and
> "onstage." When she speaks, she doesn't need to
> be fully seen from "backstage," but maybe she is
> partly seen through the curtain, depending on
> how the "backstage" and "onstage" effects are
> achieved. She is clearly heard.)*

BRITNEY
("Onstage" as THE NARRATOR.)

"Welcome to our little corner of the world.
We find ourselves at the turn of the year.
Which year? You might ask.
Now, see, the calendar's a funny thing..."

> *(CAITLIN is wide-eyed.)*

SM/ASM

And then Caitlin time traveled.

*(STUDENTS hum a single drawn out note that
cuts off just after the first line of the next scene.)*

<u>ACT 2 / SCENE 12 - Opening Night, On Stage</u>
Location: The Stage

*[NOTE: This scene could be very cheesy if not
done well. It is the climax of the show and needs
to be electrically charged to work. Take the time
to find the emotional arc as an ensemble and
make sure the timing and blocking is well
rehearsed, but feels organic and spontaneous.]*

*(Lights have shifted dramatically in a fluid
moment. It is somewhere in the middle of the
final scene of the play. CAITLIN is barefoot,
wears a night dress that hangs just below her
knees. She should have blood on her dress (and
possibly her hands if you can achieve it), as she
has just killed THE LOVE INTEREST. She could
be carrying a dirty shovel, but it's not necessary.
The lighting is shadowy moonlight, brightest on
CAITLIN, who is clearly visible centered
"onstage." Some light falling snow would be
lovely here, but not necessary. SCOTTY could be
in the very background, sprawled on the
ground.)*

SM

She found herself in the middle of the play's final scene
where she has just killed her husband.

*(STUDENTS' hum from the previous scene ends
with a pop. Some tense ambient outdoor night
noises like crickets and owls.)*

CAITLIN

(As THE LEAD.)

"It's too soon.
It went too quickly.
Can't I change what happened?"

CYNTHIA

*(As THE LOVE INTEREST'S MOTHER, off to the side. She
is more confident than she has seemed offstage. Her
character is clearly a ghost, but not in a silly way.)*

"My dear, you can't go backwards.
I've tried. All of us have tried."

*(Gestures around her, where several additional
characters appear, also ghosts.)*

"It never works. It's never worth it."

CAITLIN

(As THE LEAD, thinking.)

"You have to know,
I loved your son dearly.
I didn't mean for this to happen."

*(If a shovel is used, CAITLIN can hand it to
CYNTHIA here.)*

CYNTHIA
(As THE LOVE INTEREST'S MOTHER.)

"I know you did. I saw it from here.
And he knew too. It was an accident."

CAITLIN
*(As THE LEAD, holding her stomach where she realizes she
is wounded.)*

"Why isn't he here with me?
I don't want to go alone."

CYNTHIA
(As THE LOVE INTEREST'S MOTHER.)

"He'll be along soon. Not to worry.
Something like this can't be rushed.
You know how much he loved life."

CAITLIN
(As THE LEAD, pleading.)

"I didn't know life could take so long."

> *(All stage lights go out on "so long," and if
> possible, all lights in the theatre. It is as dark as
> possible. Any music/sound effects should also
> disappear.)*

SM
*(Immediately and with authority - the audience needs to be
assured that the power out is part of the play.)*
And then the power went out. Caitlin stood in the darkness,
unsure of what to do. *(SM clicks on a bright red flashlight.)*
Ms. Mae had prepared them for many things, but a power
out was not one of them. *(She shines it all around, including*

SM (cont)
across the audience.) The only sound was a collective breath
held as the audience, cast, and crew waited for what came
next.

ASM

In an instant, with raw instinct, Caitlin raised her hands in
front of her, grasping for whatever might be ahead. An
unseen veil. A moment hovering on the edge. The fragile
gauze between this life and the next hung invisible before
her. One of her lines fell into place.

CAITLIN

(As THE LEAD, searching.)

"Mother. Mother!
I found my watch.
It was here the whole time."

SM

(Clears her throat. Encourages NORA to step forward.)
Nora stepped forward to move the scene along.

NORA

*(As THE LEAD'S MOTHER, steps forward but isn't fully
seen in the light.)*

"I knew you would, honey.
You always did."

SETH

*(Joins in costume as THE NEWSPAPER BOY, but not in
character. Removes his hat.)*
A few others joined, standing next to Nora, understanding
that they would all continue through the technical glitch,
because that's just what needed to be done.

TEAGAN
(In costume as THE MILKMAN, but not in character.)
The audience seemed to have disappeared, evaporated in the
dark.

OLIVIA
(In costume as THE SCIENTIST, but not in character.)
Caitlin skipped ahead in the script.

CAITLIN
(As THE LEAD.)

"There's nothing I want more than to know you all again.
To start over.
To know *all* of it."

> *(ASM clicks on a blue flashlight. It should
> combine with the red flashlight to form a patchy
> purple wash.)*

CAITLIN
(As THE LEAD.)

"For the split second we have together
I'd like to really see you."

NORA
*(In costume as THE LEAD'S MOTHER, but no longer in
character.)*
And Caitlin turned her head to the side where she knew
Britney should be:

CAITLIN
(As THE LEAD.)

"It isn't supposed to end like this.
Can I try again so I can enjoy every last crumb of it?

CAITLIN (cont)
I don't want to make the same mistakes."

OLIVIA
(In costume as THE MILKMAN, but not in character.)
Britney, as The Narrator, stepped into the dim light.

BRITNEY
(Stepping forward as THE NARRATOR.)

"We can't go backwards.
We can only move forward."

CYNTHIA
*(In costume as THE LOVE INTEREST'S MOTHER, but not
in character until her line in the play.)*
A pause and then Cynthia skipped ahead, eager to prove
herself further. *(Steps forward.)*

"It's lovely tonight.
It's brisk out, almost as if we're stepping into…"

JACOB
*(In costume as THE TENNIS PLAYER, but not in character
until he says the line he steals.)*
Interrupting with the middle of someone else's line, Jacob
projected:

"…an era of uncertainty."

SM

A pause, and then…

SCOTTY
*(In costume as THE LOVE INTEREST, but not in character.
Steps forward.)*
…a week and a half of incredible work paying off, Britney,
now really and truly The Narrator, took control of the final
moments with the required ease of someone who had been
around for a very long time.

BRITNEY
(In character as THE NARRATOR.)

"It *is* brisk out tonight. I should have brought a sweater.
Even a scarf would have been a good idea.
No matter how hard we try, we're never really ready, are we?

The seasons change while we're looking the other way.
Summer falls asleep and leaves gather at the corner of the
street.
Soon the edges of our gravestones are rounded off with snow
and it's like we were never even here.
It's not the universe that asks us the question,
it's something we must ask of ourselves:
'What exactly is the point of our time here?'"

CYNTHIA
*(In costume as THE LOVE INTEREST'S MOTHER, but not
in character.)*
And it was at this moment that Caitlin realized…

SETH
*(In costume as THE NEWSPAPER BOY, but not in
character.)*
…with her hands stretched out into the darkness…

SCOTTY
(In costume as THE LOVE INTEREST, but not in character.)
…that she was actually *not* in a play…

HARLOW
*(Joins from offstage as themself, wearing something nice The
House Manager would wear. Puts their arm through
SCOTTY's and lays their head on his shoulder. [Change
"Friday" to whatever night the performance is on.])*
…standing on a stage in a small town high school on a
Friday night…

LEVI
*(Joins from the audience as himself, sits on the edge of the
stage and illuminates from below with his cellphone.)*
…but rather, at the top of a hill covered in grass at the very
edge of the galaxy, a trillion billion light years from earth.

BRITNEY
*(In costume as THE NARRATOR, but not in character. She
crouches down and puts her arm around LEVI, who looks at
her and grins.)*
Her feet were sore and sunk down into several inches of mud
and she was the happiest she had ever been. She repeated,
with absolute certainty, and to no one in particular:

CAITLIN
(In costume and character as THE LEAD.)

"There's nothing I want more than to know you all again.
To start over.
To know *all* of it."

(Pause.)

SM
The lights clicked off in almost perfect unison.

(The flashlights turn off, but not LEVI's phone.)

CAITLIN/BRITNEY

(Not in character, but also not totally themselves.)
And a silence stretched on for possibly eternity.

(LEVI's phone light goes out. A pause before moving on softly to the next scene. It should be clear that The Winter Play *is over.)*

ACT 2 / SCENE 13 - Cardboard
Location: MS. MAE's apartment

(The large "murder board" is in the background. ASM stands center stage holding a giant stack of cardboard recycling. From the top of the pile, she holds up the cardboard sign that says "The Theatre Teacher's Home." ASM then adds the sign back to the stack she is holding. MS. MAE walks to center stage in pajamas and a purple bathrobe, and starts tying up two giant bags of trash. SM joins with a cardboard sign that says "Sunday Night" then adds it to ASM's pile.)

ASM
It was late on Sunday night.

(SM starts breaking down a couple of boxes during the scene and adding them to ASM's pile.)

SM
The show was over. And Ms. Mae could attempt to return to life as a normal human adult.

ASM

The fridge remained empty.

SM

The laundry was sorted, but still a day or two away from getting washed.

MS. MAE
(Looking around, frazzled.)
I need to grade some papers.

ASM
(To MS. MAE.)
You could take a second.

MS. MAE
(Picks up a stack of new scripts.)
I could… re-read the spring musical and make sure I picked the right one.

SM
(To MS. MAE.)
Take a minute, I dare you.

(MS. MAE looks back at her "murder board" longingly.)

MS. MAE
Go with your gut.… I could…

(Maybe she takes CAITLIN's photo down and looks at it. ASM hands MS. MAE the stack of recycling.)

MS. MAE/SM/ASM
Go take the recycling out.

(MS. MAE walks off stage with the stack of recycling.)

<u>ACT 2 / SCENE 14 - Purple</u>
Location: Car, Hallway

(Blank stage. Everything in this scene should echo the first scene of the show. The narration should match the action. EVERYONE should be out of their The Winter Play *costumes and into their everyday clothes.)*

SM
Caitlin Gutierrez climbed out of the middle seat of her parents' candy apple red minivan at the front of school. She pulled her side bag across a sweatshirt she had gotten for her birthday, but never worn. It was purple and made her feel kinda like a gumdrop, but that was okay.

ASM
Seth waited for Caitlin right inside the front door because it really was too cold to wait outside and she didn't blame him.

(SETH's jaw drops when he sees CAITLIN in the purple sweatshirt.)

SETH
Where did this come from!?

CAITLIN
My aunt. She doesn't really know my *aesthetic*.

SETH

(Mocking, smiling.)
Aesthetic.

CAITLIN

Saw it and it's not the worst, so - I figured I'd try something
new.

> *(LEVI walks by and rushes over to give*
> *CAITLIN a hug. And exchanges some sort of*
> *high five, bro exchange with SETH, but it doesn't*
> *totally land for either of them and they laugh it*
> *off.)*

LEVI

You both killed it. The theatre department is in good hands!

> *(SETH does an improvised NEWSPAPER BOY*
> *action like he's holding a newspaper and*
> *laughs.)*

SETH

Extry! Extry!

CAITLIN

Thanks, man! Everyone was so glad you made it to opening
night.

SETH

I heard Ms. Mae worked her magic so you could sneak in.

LEVI

You guys are my family, I wouldn't have missed it for the
world!

> *(The school bell rings. LEVI rushes off with a*
> *wave and a spin. SCOTTY and HARLOW rush*

*by in the opposite direction holding hands.
Waves are exchanged and greetings ad-libbed
between all.)*

SM
Seth grabbed Caitlin's hand and they walked to their lockers.
Caitlin unloaded her textbooks from the weekend.

*(SETH grabs a couple of books of his own and
blows CAITLIN an exaggerated kiss as he exits
for class. CAITLIN closes her locker. This can
all be mimed. Perhaps a STUDENT can be
holding up the poster.)*

SM
She looked at the poster for *The Winter Play* taped to the
outside of her locker. Someone had drawn a little star next to
her name with a highlighter. She pulled out a Sharpie and
added a tiny smiley face.

(BRITNEY joins CAITLIN.)

BRITNEY
*(It's clear BRITNEY has grown up a bit since the first scene
of the play.)*
Congrats.

*(CAITLIN glances over and meets the gaze of
someone she never knew she could like so
much.)*

CAITLIN
*(It's clear CAITLIN has grown up a lot since the first scene
of the play.)*
Britney. *(Hugs her.)* Thank you! You were so, *so* good.

BRITNEY

That was absolutely wild, yeah?

CAITLIN

So wild! Why did the power have to go out *right* then? We were so close to the end!

BRITNEY

(Laughs.)
So close! Uh - did you see what Mae just posted?

CAITLIN

No, what!?

BRITNEY

Sign ups for the musical.

(CAITLIN and BRITNEY get excited together and hype each other up. Lights out.)

ACT 2 / SCENE 15 - Twenty Something Years Later
Location: A Stage

(This scene flows as smoothly and as quickly as possible from the previous. CAITLIN has taken off her sweatshirt and wears something appropriate for a mid-thirties teacher, maybe something like a purple sport coat and a name badge hanging around her neck. STUDENTS filter in.)

SM

(Holds a sign that says "Twenty Something Years Later.")
It is twenty something years later and Caitlin waits patiently
as students sling their backpacks to the floor and settle into
the first few rows of the theatre. Excitement is in the air. Can
you feel it?

CAITLIN/MS. GUTIERREZ

(Standing at the front.)
Okay everyone, grab a seat. Let's talk about where we're
going.

After a long process, and intense debate with the music
folks, we've finally decided the shows and musical for next
year! Some of you will be *ecstatic*, and maybe a few of you
will not, but that's okay! I promise these are great shows and
you'll have a blast.

ASM

One freshman raises their hand and begins speaking
immediately.

STUDENT

I, for one, will be excited no matter the shows. I will work
hard in whatever role. It's an honor to be considered.

(Some of the STUDENTS snicker.)

CAITLIN/MS. GUTIERREZ

Thank you! I love the initiative you've got there, buddy. I'm
sure you'll be amazing! Now, for our first show, I want to
revisit a play that means a whole heck of a lot to me. It was
actually the first show I acted in.

SM

Caitlin - er - Ms. Gutierrez sits down on the edge of the stage. She takes a deep breath, surveying the eager eyes of the students she loves so dearly.

CAITLIN/MS. GUTIERREZ

The Winter Play is about time travel.

(Lights out. End of play.)

www.ingramcontent.com/pod-product-compliance
Lightning Source LLC
Chambersburg PA
CBHW022103050726
47591CB00002B/644